A Dog's Guide To Making It In America

Volume 1

Rodolfo G Ledesma

Published in the U.S.A. by the author.

Ledesma, Rodolfo G.

A Dog's Guide to Making It in America

ISBN-10: 0984887407

ISBN-13: 978-0-9848874-0-8

Printed in the U.S.A.

Cover design and illustrations by the author.

First Edition

For my mom, Emma

And in loving memomery of my dad, Enrique

Contents

Obedience School

Somewhere in the outskirts of Manila, sometime in the not-so-distant future, . . .

AMERICA IS A MELTING POT, BUT AS AN *IMMIGRANT* DOG, YOU DON'T WANT TO LOSE YOUR OWN CULTURE'S UNIQUENESS.

MY FATHER WAS AN AMERICAN LABRADOR, AND MY MOTHER, SHE CAME FROM MANILA, WHERE I WAS BORN. THEN WE IMMIGRATED TO AMERICA.

LIKE MANY IMMIGRANTS DOGS BROUGHT UP IN AMERICA, I CONSIDERED MYSELF PRETTY MUCH AN AMERICAN.

BUT WHEN IT CAME TIME TO FILLING OUT THE *FINANCIAL AID* FORM IN OBEDIENCE SCHOOL, I WAS A *PACIFIC ISLANDER* DOG.

EARLY ON THE CURRICULUM WAS THIN, NOT BECAUSE AT THE TIME OBEDIENCE SCHOOLS DID NOT HAVE ANYTHING LIKE THE *NO DOG LEFT BEHIND* LAW.

THE HUMAN TRAINERS FOCUSED ON TEACHING YOU SIMPLE COMMANDS LIKE "SIT" AND "STAY," BUT MOSTLY "FETCH."

LATER ON WE HAD LOTS OF TRAINING ON ACTION FOLLOWED BY REWARD, LIKE BARK THREE TIMES, THEN GET FOOD REWARD. YOUR BASIC *PAVLOVIAN* STUFF.

HOW DO YOU KNOW IF YOU'RE GOOD, OR BETTER THAN THE OTHER DOG?

I WAS ON FINANCIAL AID, SO I WAS HANDICAPPED FROM THE GET-GO.

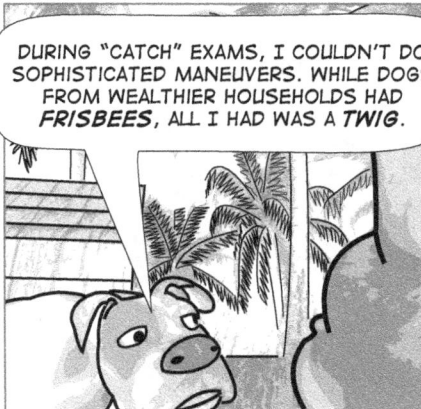

DURING "CATCH" EXAMS, I COULDN'T DO SOPHISTICATED MANEUVERS. WHILE DOGS FROM WEALTHIER HOUSEHOLDS HAD *FRISBEES*, ALL I HAD WAS A *TWIG*.

YOU HAD TO HAVE A FRISBEE TO MAKE *DEAN'S LIST*.

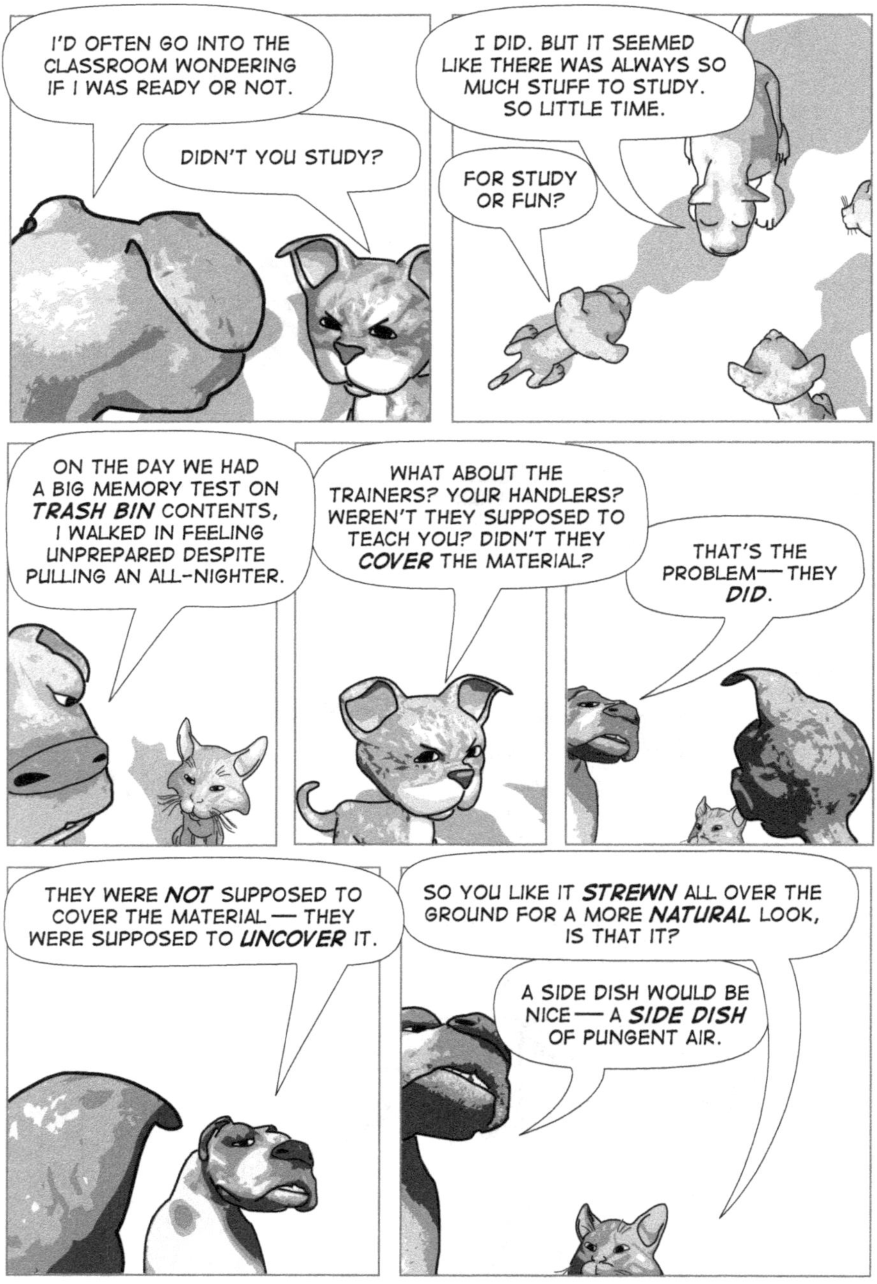
I'D OFTEN GO INTO THE CLASSROOM WONDERING IF I WAS READY OR NOT.
DIDN'T YOU STUDY?
I DID. BUT IT SEEMED LIKE THERE WAS ALWAYS SO MUCH STUFF TO STUDY. SO LITTLE TIME.
FOR STUDY OR FUN?
ON THE DAY WE HAD A BIG MEMORY TEST ON ***TRASH BIN*** CONTENTS, I WALKED IN FEELING UNPREPARED DESPITE PULLING AN ALL-NIGHTER.
WHAT ABOUT THE TRAINERS? YOUR HANDLERS? WEREN'T THEY SUPPOSED TO TEACH YOU? DIDN'T THEY ***COVER*** THE MATERIAL?
THAT'S THE PROBLEM— THEY ***DID***.
THEY WERE ***NOT*** SUPPOSED TO COVER THE MATERIAL — THEY WERE SUPPOSED TO ***UNCOVER*** IT.
SO YOU LIKE IT ***STREWN*** ALL OVER THE GROUND FOR A MORE ***NATURAL*** LOOK, IS THAT IT?
A SIDE DISH WOULD BE NICE — A ***SIDE DISH*** OF PUNGENT AIR.

Campus Meal Plans

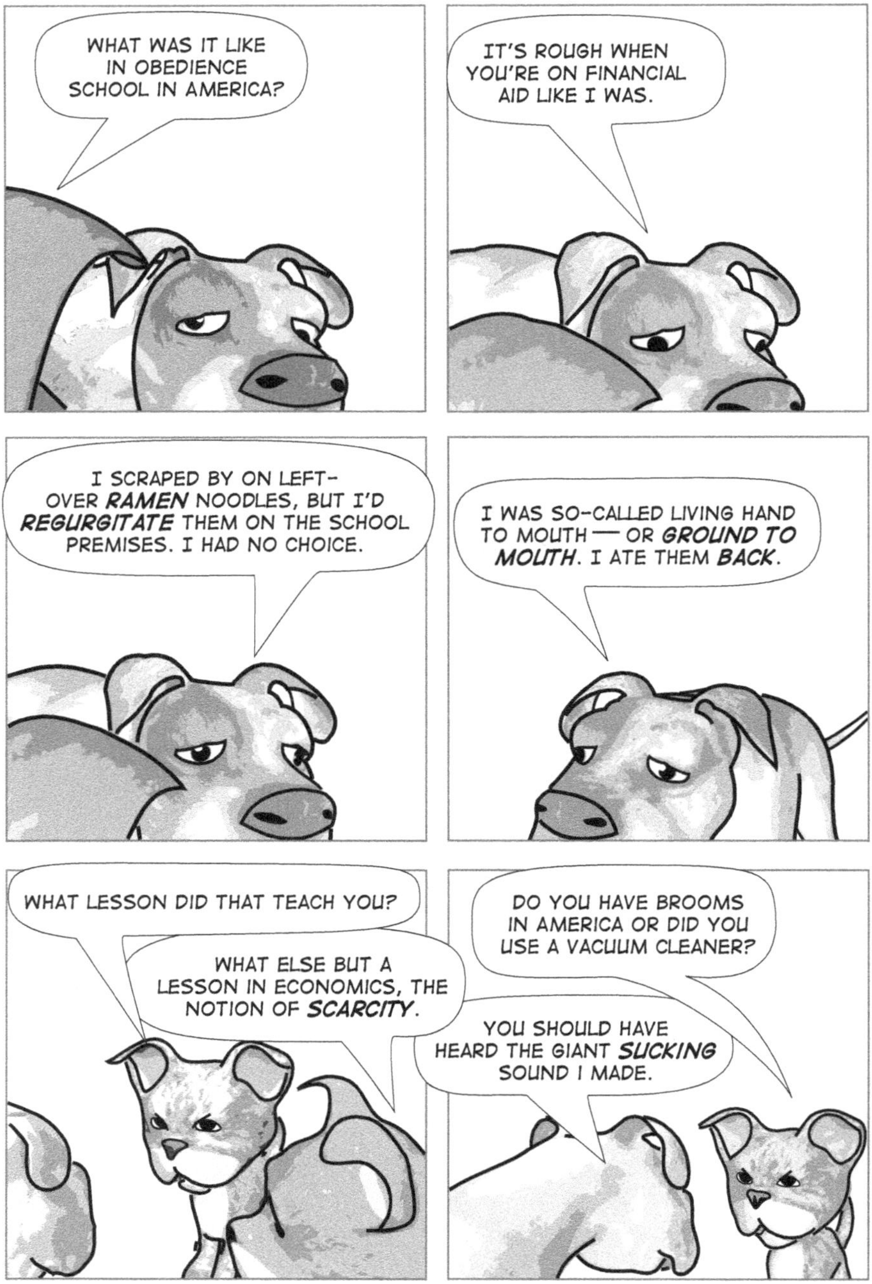
WHAT WAS IT LIKE IN OBEDIENCE SCHOOL IN AMERICA?
IT'S ROUGH WHEN YOU'RE ON FINANCIAL AID LIKE I WAS.
I SCRAPED BY ON LEFT-OVER RAMEN NOODLES, BUT I'D REGURGITATE THEM ON THE SCHOOL PREMISES. I HAD NO CHOICE.
I WAS SO-CALLED LIVING HAND TO MOUTH — OR GROUND TO MOUTH. I ATE THEM BACK.
WHAT LESSON DID THAT TEACH YOU?
WHAT ELSE BUT A LESSON IN ECONOMICS, THE NOTION OF SCARCITY.
DO YOU HAVE BROOMS IN AMERICA OR DID YOU USE A VACUUM CLEANER?
YOU SHOULD HAVE HEARD THE GIANT SUCKING SOUND I MADE.

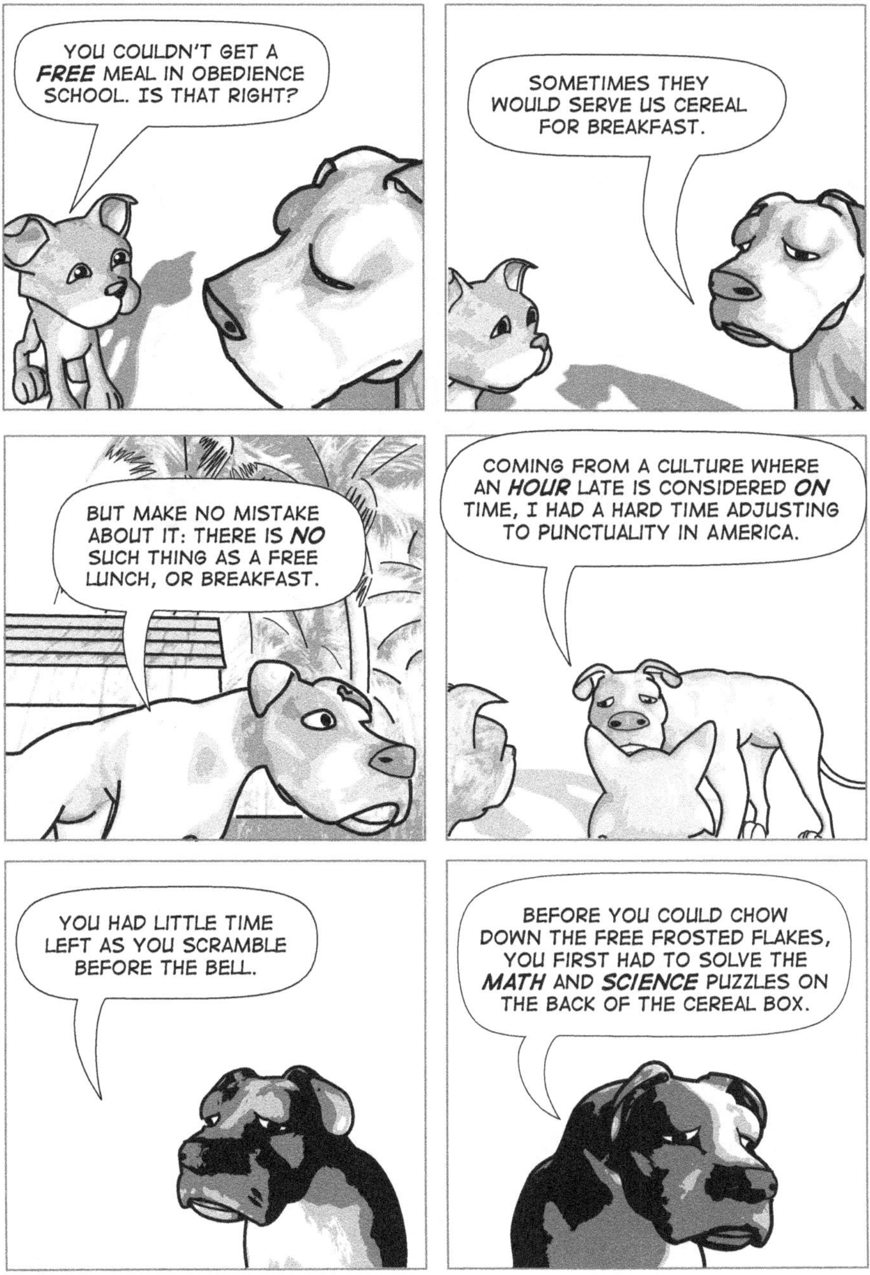
YOU COULDN'T GET A FREE MEAL IN OBEDIENCE SCHOOL. IS THAT RIGHT?
SOMETIMES THEY WOULD SERVE US CEREAL FOR BREAKFAST.
BUT MAKE NO MISTAKE ABOUT IT: THERE IS NO SUCH THING AS A FREE LUNCH, OR BREAKFAST.
COMING FROM A CULTURE WHERE AN HOUR LATE IS CONSIDERED ON TIME, I HAD A HARD TIME ADJUSTING TO PUNCTUALITY IN AMERICA.
YOU HAD LITTLE TIME LEFT AS YOU SCRAMBLE BEFORE THE BELL.
BEFORE YOU COULD CHOW DOWN THE FREE FROSTED FLAKES, YOU FIRST HAD TO SOLVE THE MATH AND SCIENCE PUZZLES ON THE BACK OF THE CEREAL BOX.

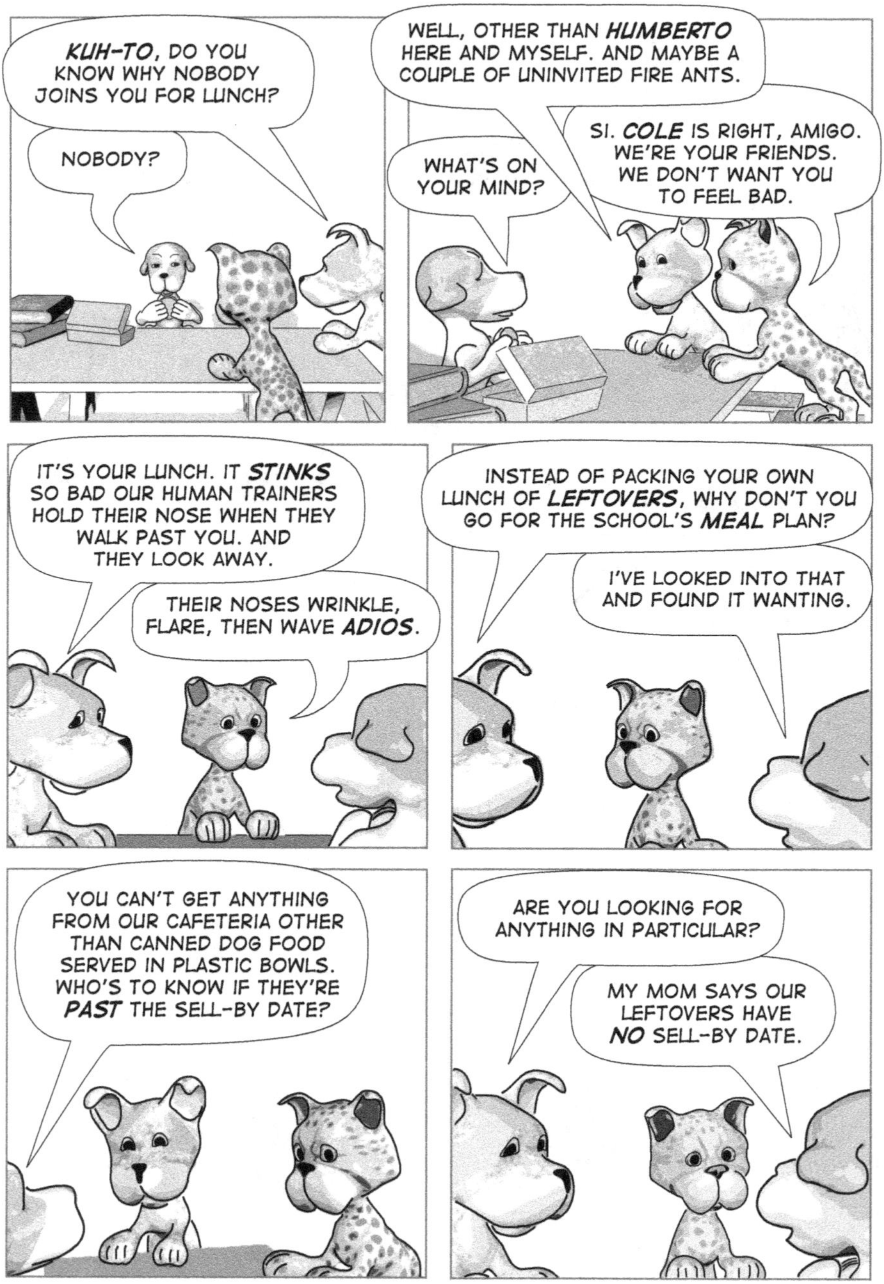
KUH-TO, DO YOU KNOW WHY NOBODY JOINS YOU FOR LUNCH?
NOBODY?
WELL, OTHER THAN HUMBERTO HERE AND MYSELF. AND MAYBE A COUPLE OF UNINVITED FIRE ANTS.
WHAT'S ON YOUR MIND?
SI. COLE IS RIGHT, AMIGO. WE'RE YOUR FRIENDS. WE DON'T WANT YOU TO FEEL BAD.
IT'S YOUR LUNCH. IT STINKS SO BAD OUR HUMAN TRAINERS HOLD THEIR NOSE WHEN THEY WALK PAST YOU. AND THEY LOOK AWAY.
THEIR NOSES WRINKLE, FLARE, THEN WAVE ADIOS.
INSTEAD OF PACKING YOUR OWN LUNCH OF LEFTOVERS, WHY DON'T YOU GO FOR THE SCHOOL'S MEAL PLAN?
I'VE LOOKED INTO THAT AND FOUND IT WANTING.
YOU CAN'T GET ANYTHING FROM OUR CAFETERIA OTHER THAN CANNED DOG FOOD SERVED IN PLASTIC BOWLS. WHO'S TO KNOW IF THEY'RE PAST THE SELL-BY DATE?
ARE YOU LOOKING FOR ANYTHING IN PARTICULAR?
MY MOM SAYS OUR LEFTOVERS HAVE NO SELL-BY DATE.

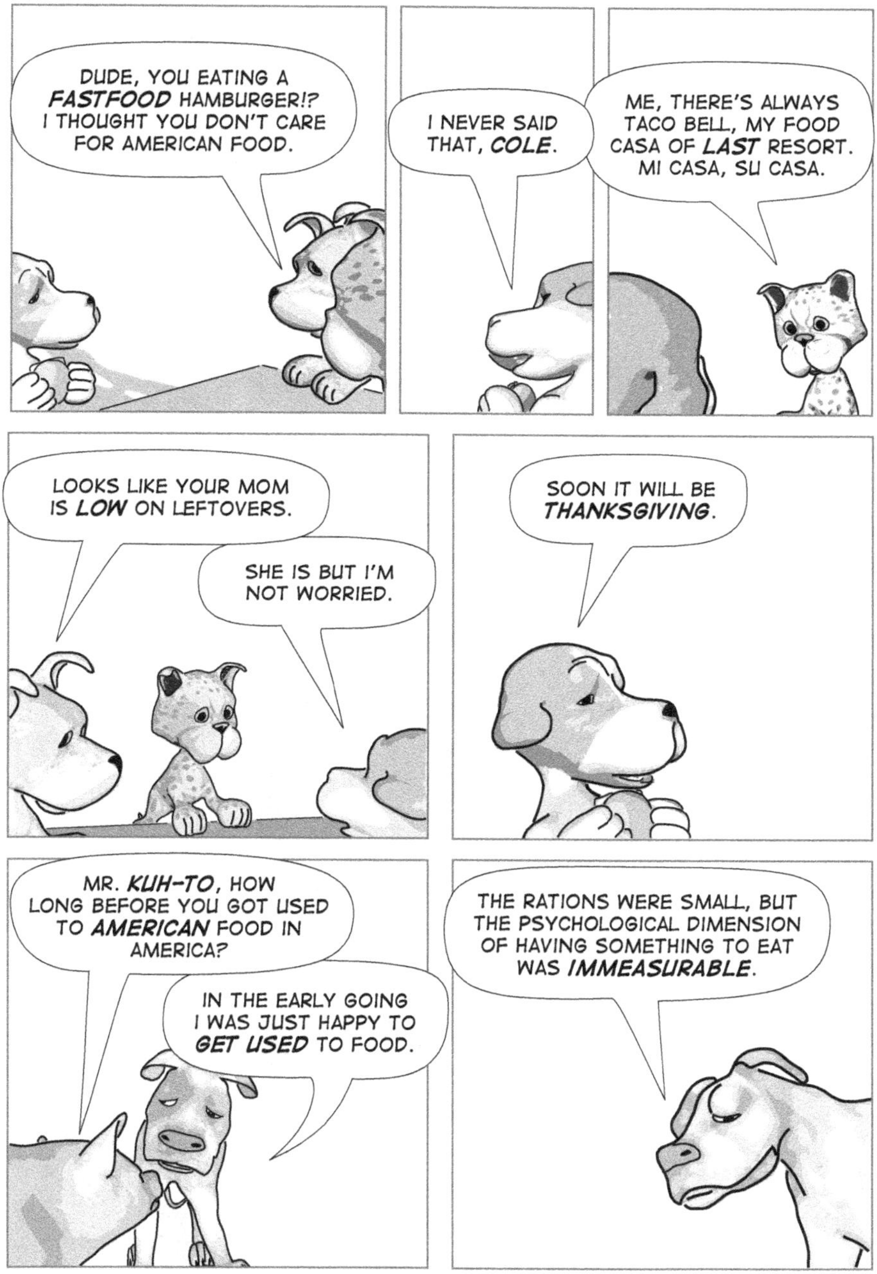
DUDE, YOU EATING A *FASTFOOD* HAMBURGER!? I THOUGHT YOU DON'T CARE FOR AMERICAN FOOD.
I NEVER SAID THAT, *COLE*.
ME, THERE'S ALWAYS TACO BELL, MY FOOD CASA OF *LAST* RESORT. MI CASA, SU CASA.
LOOKS LIKE YOUR MOM IS *LOW* ON LEFTOVERS.
SHE IS BUT I'M NOT WORRIED.
SOON IT WILL BE *THANKSGIVING*.
MR. *KUH-TO*, HOW LONG BEFORE YOU GOT USED TO *AMERICAN* FOOD IN AMERICA?
IN THE EARLY GOING I WAS JUST HAPPY TO *GET USED* TO FOOD.
THE RATIONS WERE SMALL, BUT THE PSYCHOLOGICAL DIMENSION OF HAVING SOMETHING TO EAT WAS *IMMEASURABLE*.

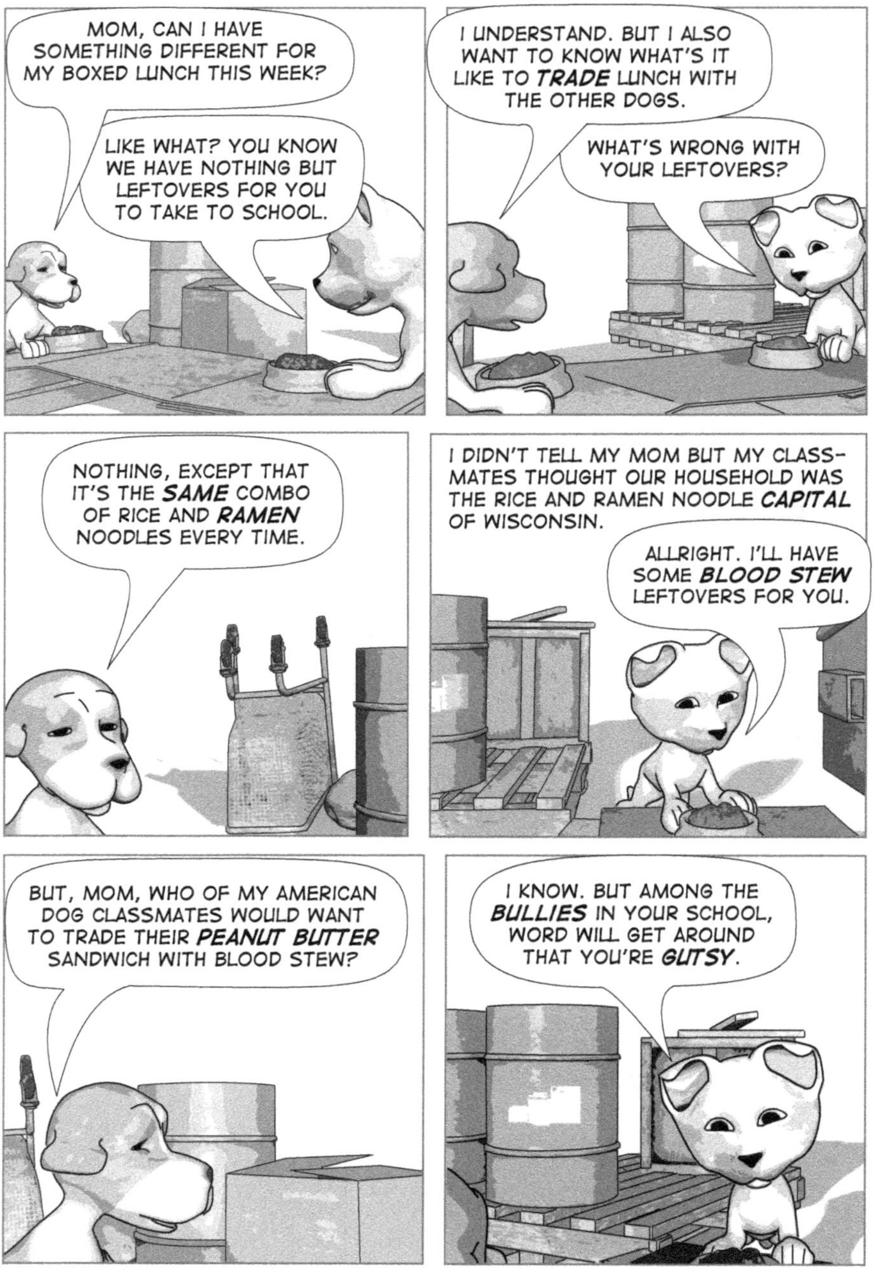
MOM, CAN I HAVE SOMETHING DIFFERENT FOR MY BOXED LUNCH THIS WEEK?
LIKE WHAT? YOU KNOW WE HAVE NOTHING BUT LEFTOVERS FOR YOU TO TAKE TO SCHOOL.
I UNDERSTAND. BUT I ALSO WANT TO KNOW WHAT'S IT LIKE TO *TRADE* LUNCH WITH THE OTHER DOGS.
WHAT'S WRONG WITH YOUR LEFTOVERS?
NOTHING, EXCEPT THAT IT'S THE *SAME* COMBO OF RICE AND *RAMEN* NOODLES EVERY TIME.
I DIDN'T TELL MY MOM BUT MY CLASS-MATES THOUGHT OUR HOUSEHOLD WAS THE RICE AND RAMEN NOODLE *CAPITAL* OF WISCONSIN.
ALLRIGHT. I'LL HAVE SOME *BLOOD STEW* LEFTOVERS FOR YOU.
BUT, MOM, WHO OF MY AMERICAN DOG CLASSMATES WOULD WANT TO TRADE THEIR *PEANUT BUTTER* SANDWICH WITH BLOOD STEW?
I KNOW. BUT AMONG THE *BULLIES* IN YOUR SCHOOL, WORD WILL GET AROUND THAT YOU'RE *GUTSY*.

Reading Lists

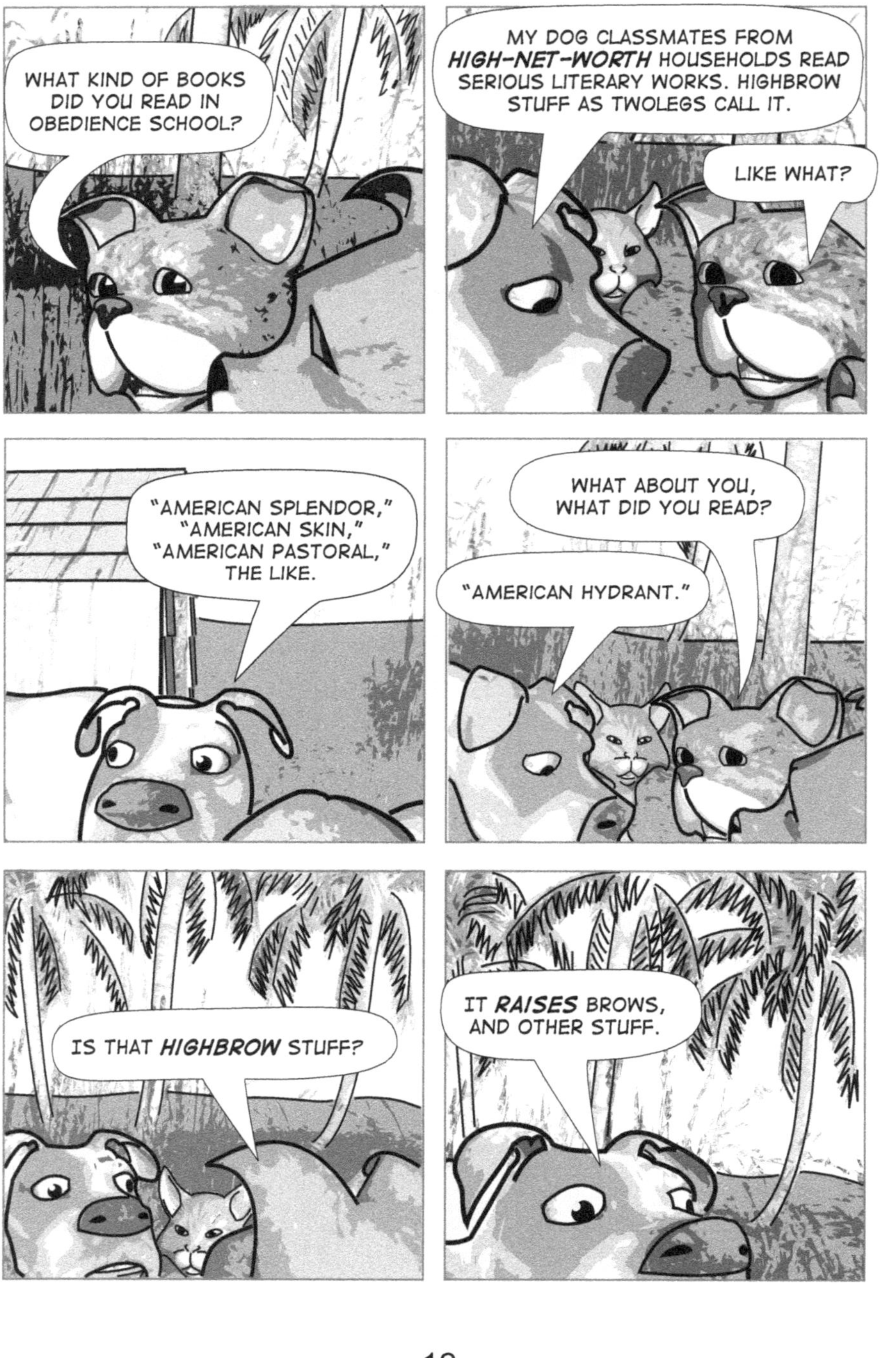
WHAT KIND OF BOOKS DID YOU READ IN OBEDIENCE SCHOOL?
MY DOG CLASSMATES FROM ***HIGH-NET-WORTH*** HOUSEHOLDS READ SERIOUS LITERARY WORKS. HIGHBROW STUFF AS TWOLEGS CALL IT.
LIKE WHAT?
"AMERICAN SPLENDOR," "AMERICAN SKIN," "AMERICAN PASTORAL," THE LIKE.
WHAT ABOUT YOU, WHAT DID YOU READ?
"AMERICAN HYDRANT."
IS THAT ***HIGHBROW*** STUFF?
IT ***RAISES*** BROWS, AND OTHER STUFF.

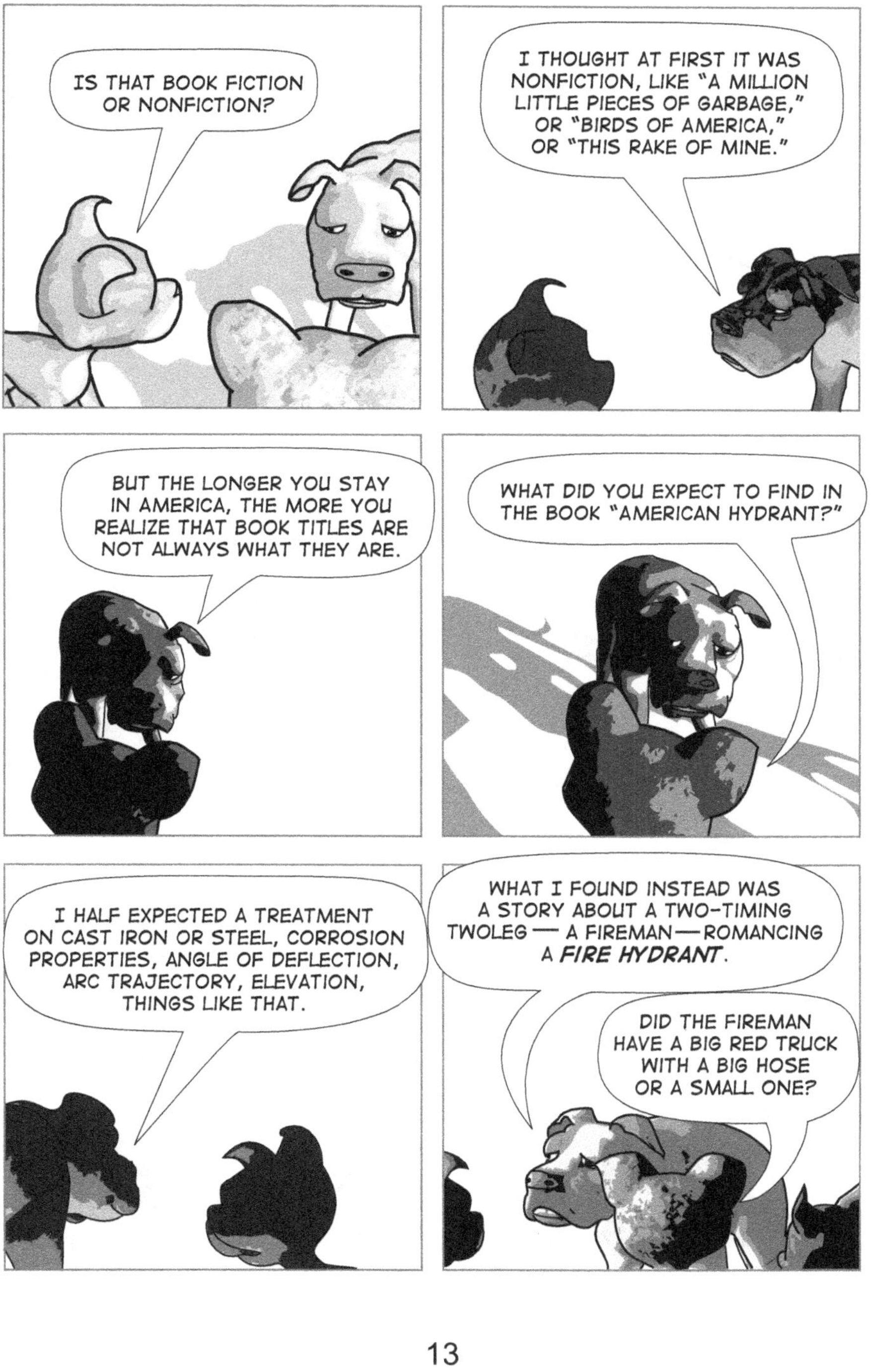
IS THAT BOOK FICTION OR NONFICTION?
I THOUGHT AT FIRST IT WAS NONFICTION, LIKE "A MILLION LITTLE PIECES OF GARBAGE," OR "BIRDS OF AMERICA," OR "THIS RAKE OF MINE."
BUT THE LONGER YOU STAY IN AMERICA, THE MORE YOU REALIZE THAT BOOK TITLES ARE NOT ALWAYS WHAT THEY ARE.
WHAT DID YOU EXPECT TO FIND IN THE BOOK "AMERICAN HYDRANT?"
I HALF EXPECTED A TREATMENT ON CAST IRON OR STEEL, CORROSION PROPERTIES, ANGLE OF DEFLECTION, ARC TRAJECTORY, ELEVATION, THINGS LIKE THAT.
WHAT I FOUND INSTEAD WAS A STORY ABOUT A TWO-TIMING TWOLEG — A FIREMAN — ROMANCING A ***FIRE HYDRANT***.
DID THE FIREMAN HAVE A BIG RED TRUCK WITH A BIG HOSE OR A SMALL ONE?

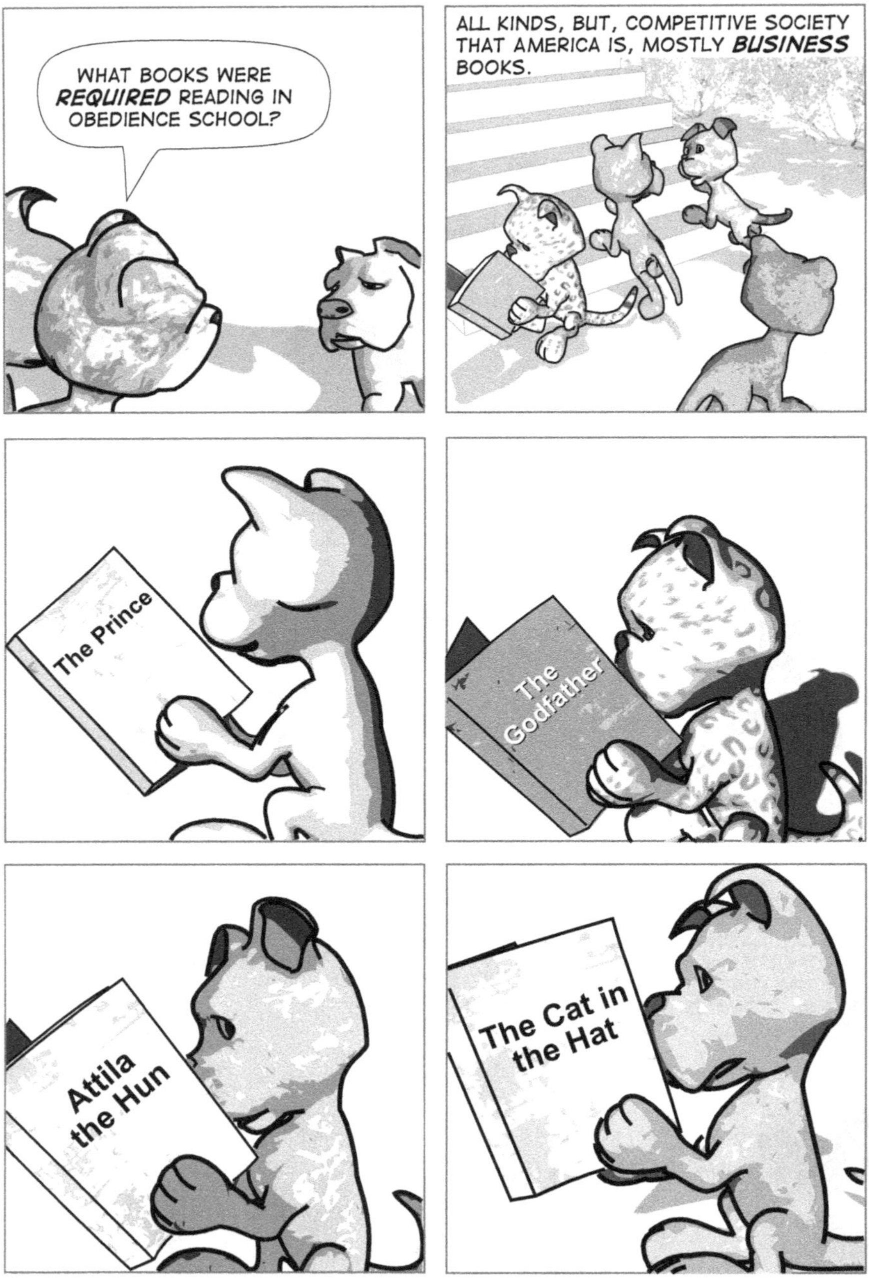
WHAT BOOKS WERE *REQUIRED* READING IN OBEDIENCE SCHOOL?
ALL KINDS, BUT, COMPETITIVE SOCIETY THAT AMERICA IS, MOSTLY *BUSINESS* BOOKS.
The Prince
The Godfather
Attila the Hun
The Cat in the Hat

MR. *KUH-TO*, DID YOUR MOM READ TO YOU WHEN YOU WERE LITTLE TO PREPARE YOU EARLY FOR SUCCESS IN DOG SCHOOL?
YES. LIKE HER HUMAN PARENT COUNTERPARTS IN AMERICA, MY MOTHER SUBSCRIBED TO THE SAME PRINCIPLE.
WHAT KIND OF BOOKS DID YOUR MOM READ TO YOU?
TRAVEL BOOKS. ONE TITLE I REMEMBER WAS "ONE THOUSAND AND ONE LANDFILLS TO VISIT BEFORE YOU DIE."
DID YOU LIKE THE BOOK?
I LOVED IT. IT WAS *TRASHY*.

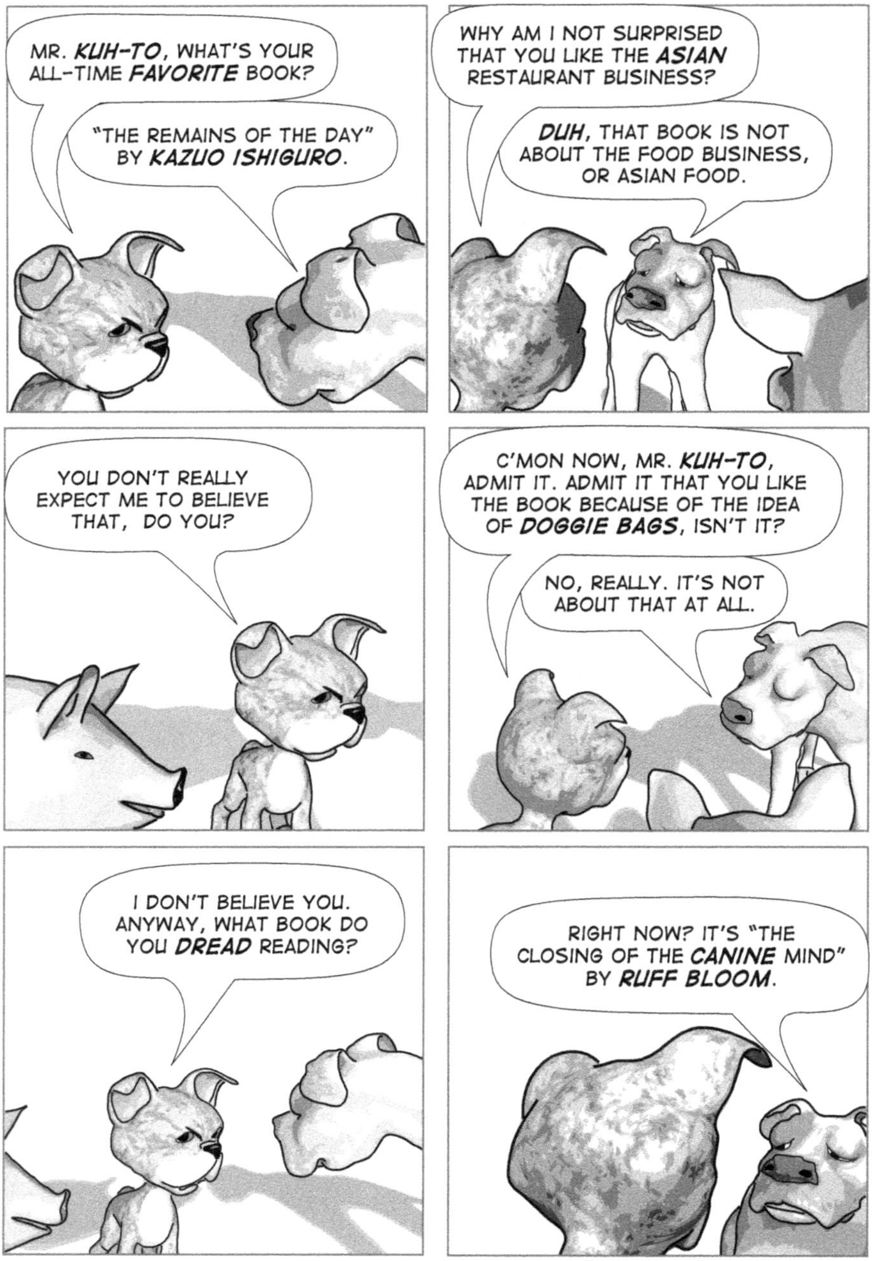
MR. KUH-TO, WHAT'S YOUR ALL-TIME FAVORITE BOOK?
"THE REMAINS OF THE DAY" BY KAZUO ISHIGURO.
WHY AM I NOT SURPRISED THAT YOU LIKE THE ASIAN RESTAURANT BUSINESS?
DUH, THAT BOOK IS NOT ABOUT THE FOOD BUSINESS, OR ASIAN FOOD.
YOU DON'T REALLY EXPECT ME TO BELIEVE THAT, DO YOU?
C'MON NOW, MR. KUH-TO, ADMIT IT. ADMIT IT THAT YOU LIKE THE BOOK BECAUSE OF THE IDEA OF DOGGIE BAGS, ISN'T IT?
NO, REALLY. IT'S NOT ABOUT THAT AT ALL.
I DON'T BELIEVE YOU. ANYWAY, WHAT BOOK DO YOU DREAD READING?
RIGHT NOW? IT'S "THE CLOSING OF THE CANINE MIND" BY RUFF BLOOM.

Making Friends on Campus

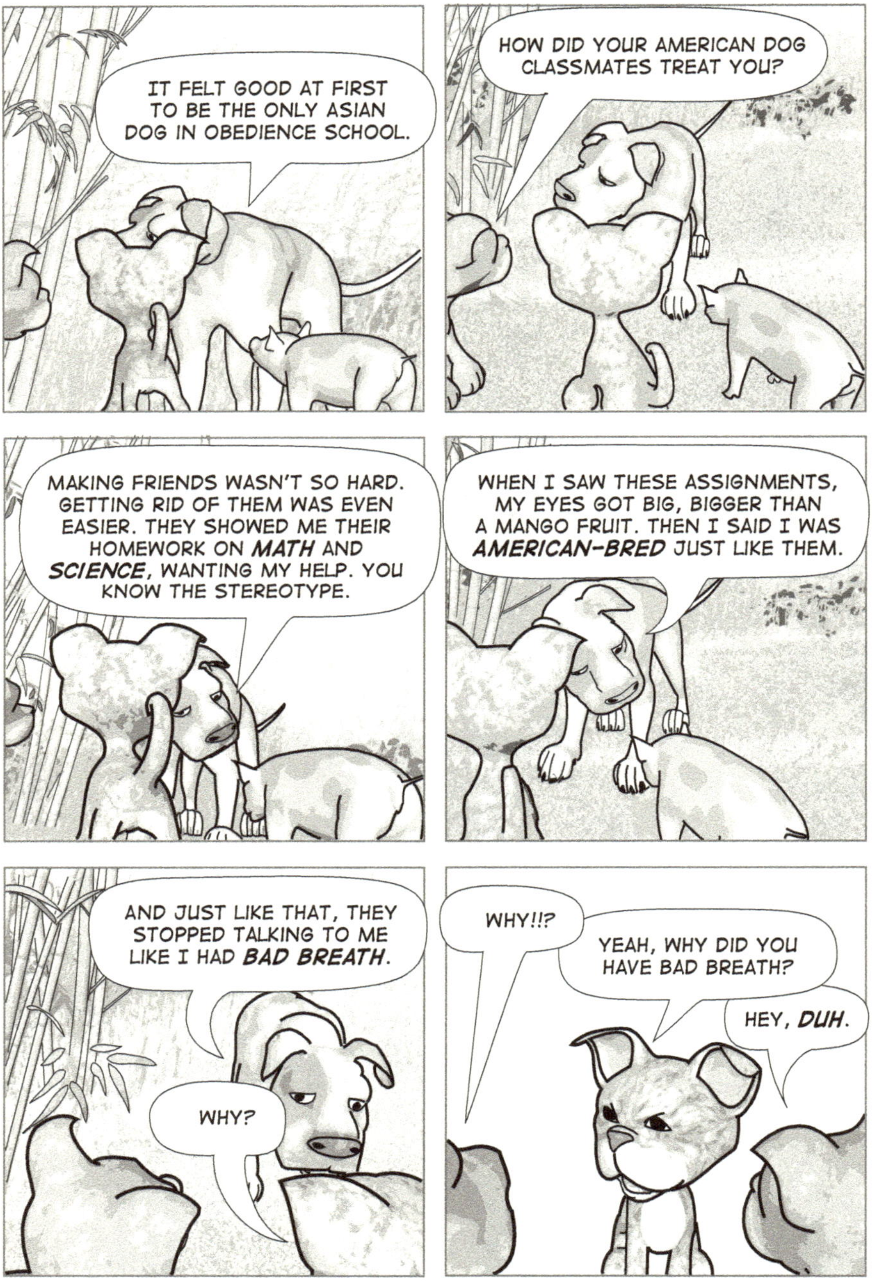
IT FELT GOOD AT FIRST TO BE THE ONLY ASIAN DOG IN OBEDIENCE SCHOOL.
HOW DID YOUR AMERICAN DOG CLASSMATES TREAT YOU?
MAKING FRIENDS WASN'T SO HARD. GETTING RID OF THEM WAS EVEN EASIER. THEY SHOWED ME THEIR HOMEWORK ON MATH AND SCIENCE, WANTING MY HELP. YOU KNOW THE STEREOTYPE.
WHEN I SAW THESE ASSIGNMENTS, MY EYES GOT BIG, BIGGER THAN A MANGO FRUIT. THEN I SAID I WAS AMERICAN-BRED JUST LIKE THEM.
AND JUST LIKE THAT, THEY STOPPED TALKING TO ME LIKE I HAD BAD BREATH.
WHY?
WHY!!?
YEAH, WHY DID YOU HAVE BAD BREATH?
HEY, DUH.

AS A NEW FOREIGN-BORN DOG ON CAMPUS, I WASN'T SURE ABOUT HOW TO GREET MY NATIVE-BORN CLASSMATES.
SO I THOUGHT I'D PLAY IT BY EAR BUT AT THE VERY LEAST, I'D BE HONEST, SINCERE.
HEY, DUDE. HOW'S IT GOING?
WELL, MY OUTLINE ON A NEW CATCH MANEUVER WAS DUE TODAY . . .
. . . BUT WHEN I GOT TO CLASS I COULDN'T FIND IT, . . .
. . . SO I ASKED THE TRAINER IF —

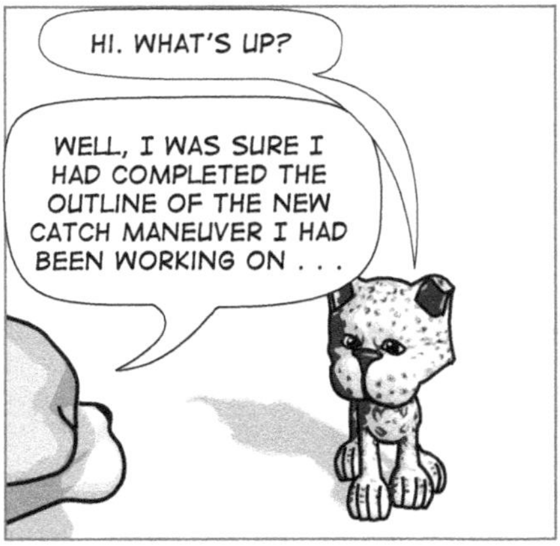
HI. WHAT'S UP?
WELL, I WAS SURE I HAD COMPLETED THE OUTLINE OF THE NEW CATCH MANEUVER I HAD BEEN WORKING ON . . .

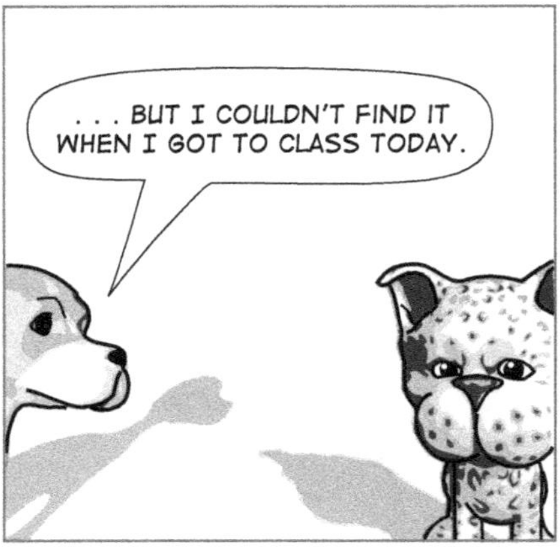
. . . BUT I COULDN'T FIND IT WHEN I GOT TO CLASS TODAY.

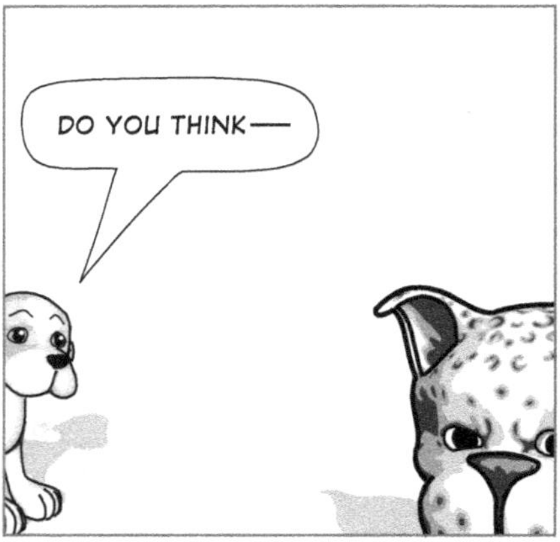
DO YOU THINK—

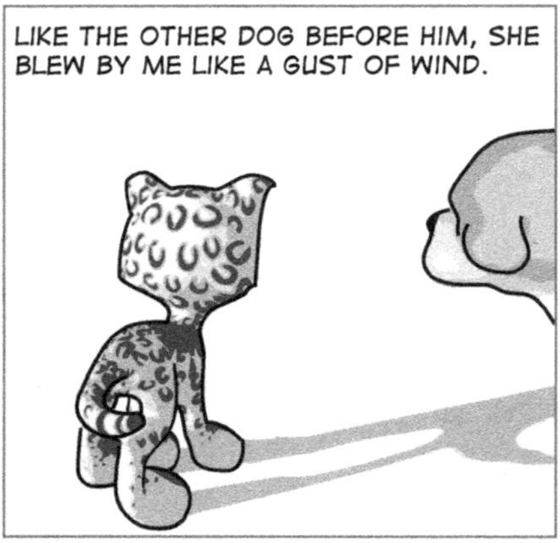
LIKE THE OTHER DOG BEFORE HIM, SHE BLEW BY ME LIKE A GUST OF WIND.

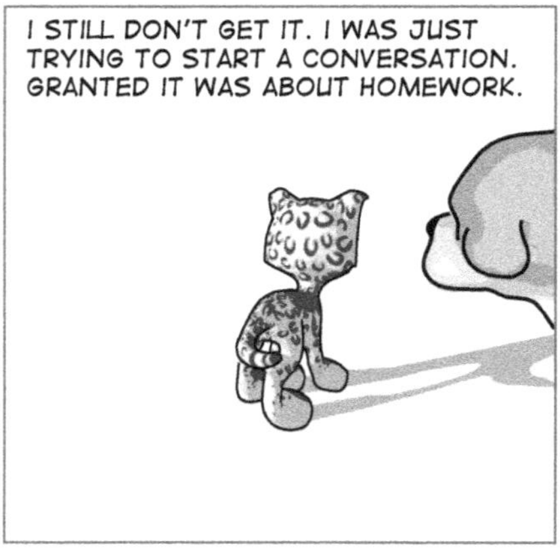
I STILL DON'T GET IT. I WAS JUST TRYING TO START A CONVERSATION. GRANTED IT WAS ABOUT HOMEWORK.

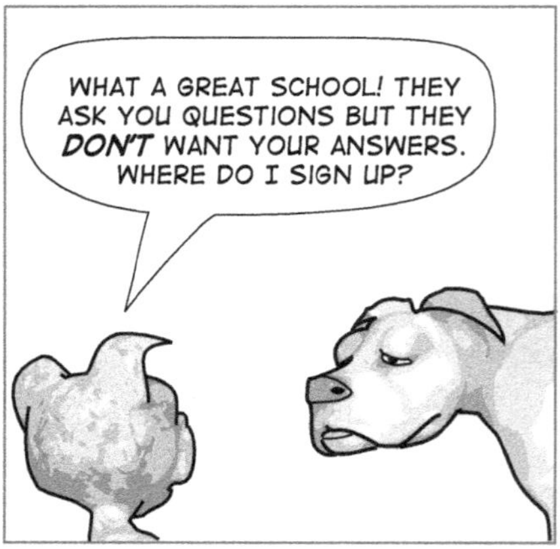
WHAT A GREAT SCHOOL! THEY ASK YOU QUESTIONS BUT THEY ***DON'T*** WANT YOUR ANSWERS. WHERE DO I SIGN UP?

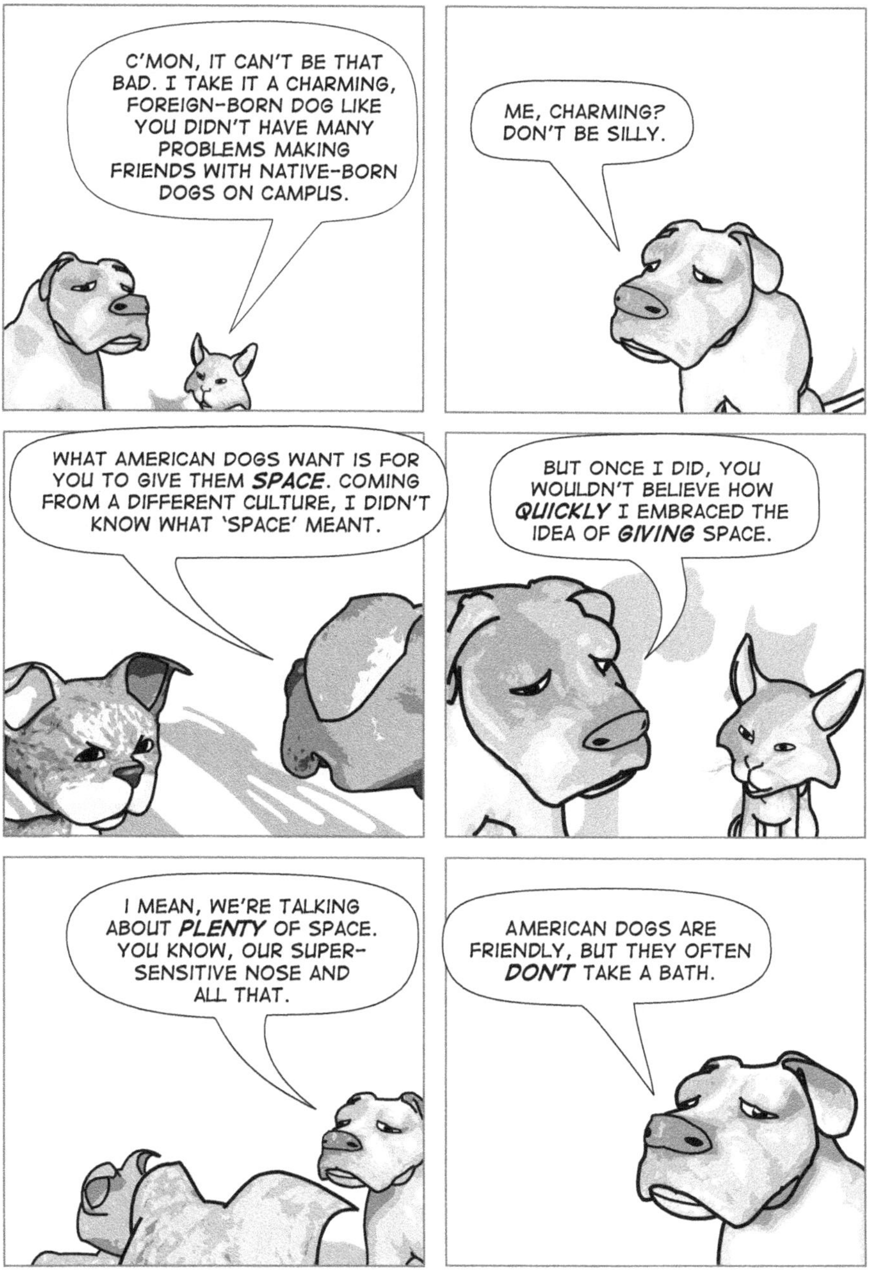
C'MON, IT CAN'T BE THAT BAD. I TAKE IT A CHARMING, FOREIGN-BORN DOG LIKE YOU DIDN'T HAVE MANY PROBLEMS MAKING FRIENDS WITH NATIVE-BORN DOGS ON CAMPUS.
ME, CHARMING? DON'T BE SILLY.
WHAT AMERICAN DOGS WANT IS FOR YOU TO GIVE THEM *SPACE*. COMING FROM A DIFFERENT CULTURE, I DIDN'T KNOW WHAT 'SPACE' MEANT.
BUT ONCE I DID, YOU WOULDN'T BELIEVE HOW *QUICKLY* I EMBRACED THE IDEA OF *GIVING* SPACE.
I MEAN, WE'RE TALKING ABOUT *PLENTY* OF SPACE. YOU KNOW, OUR SUPER-SENSITIVE NOSE AND ALL THAT.
AMERICAN DOGS ARE FRIENDLY, BUT THEY OFTEN *DON'T* TAKE A BATH.

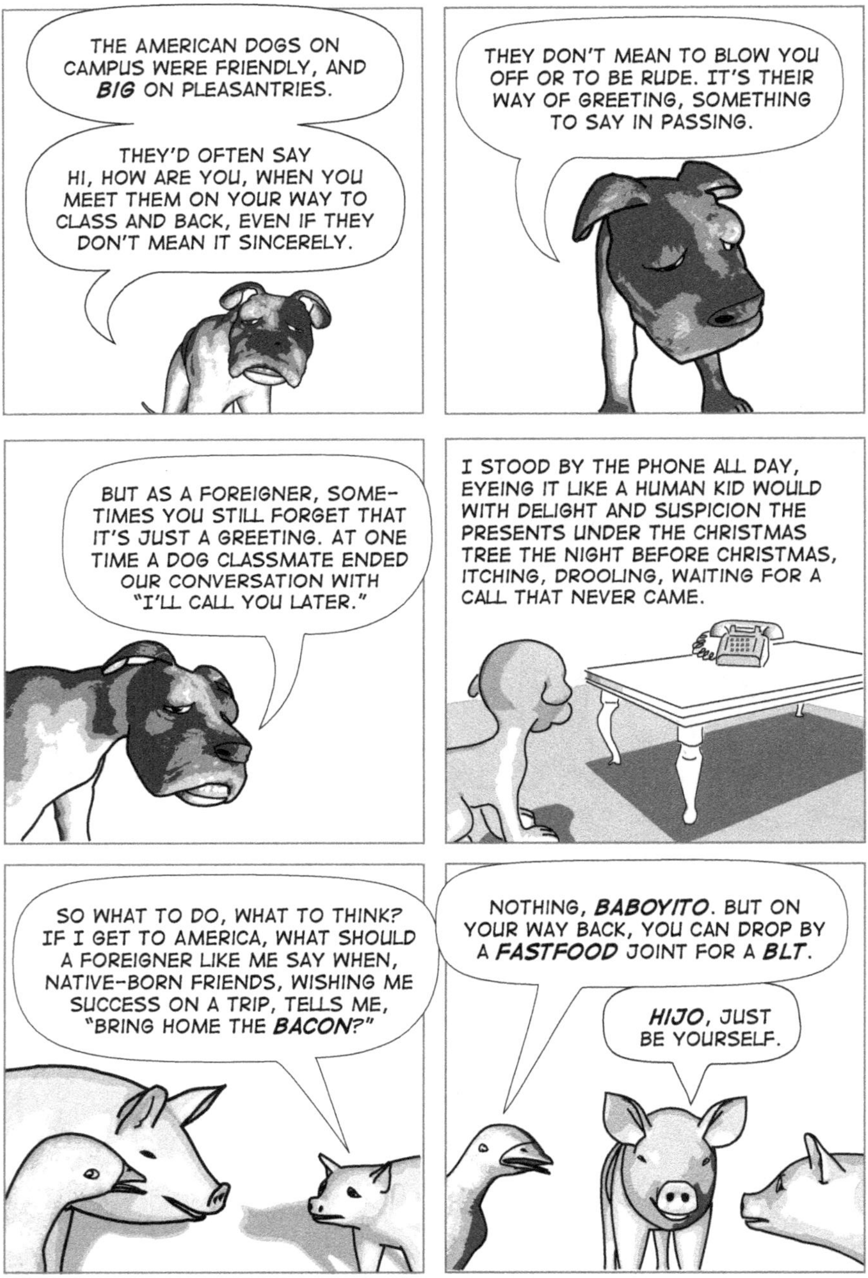
THE AMERICAN DOGS ON CAMPUS WERE FRIENDLY, AND *BIG* ON PLEASANTRIES.
THEY'D OFTEN SAY HI, HOW ARE YOU, WHEN YOU MEET THEM ON YOUR WAY TO CLASS AND BACK, EVEN IF THEY DON'T MEAN IT SINCERELY.
THEY DON'T MEAN TO BLOW YOU OFF OR TO BE RUDE. IT'S THEIR WAY OF GREETING, SOMETHING TO SAY IN PASSING.
BUT AS A FOREIGNER, SOMETIMES YOU STILL FORGET THAT IT'S JUST A GREETING. AT ONE TIME A DOG CLASSMATE ENDED OUR CONVERSATION WITH "I'LL CALL YOU LATER."
I STOOD BY THE PHONE ALL DAY, EYEING IT LIKE A HUMAN KID WOULD WITH DELIGHT AND SUSPICION THE PRESENTS UNDER THE CHRISTMAS TREE THE NIGHT BEFORE CHRISTMAS, ITCHING, DROOLING, WAITING FOR A CALL THAT NEVER CAME.
SO WHAT TO DO, WHAT TO THINK? IF I GET TO AMERICA, WHAT SHOULD A FOREIGNER LIKE ME SAY WHEN, NATIVE-BORN FRIENDS, WISHING ME SUCCESS ON A TRIP, TELLS ME, "BRING HOME THE *BACON*?"
NOTHING, ***BABOYITO***. BUT ON YOUR WAY BACK, YOU CAN DROP BY A ***FASTFOOD*** JOINT FOR A ***BLT***.
HIJO, JUST BE YOURSELF.

DID YOU HAVE TO SWEAT THE SMALL STUFF IN DOG SCHOOL?
YES.
LIKE WHAT?
OH, THE USUAL DAY-TO-DAY, FACE-TO-FACE CONVERSATIONS WITH MY AMERICAN DOG CLASSMATES.
THEY WERE NICE TO ME. BUT THEY DROOLED A LOT. GROSS.

Plagiarism

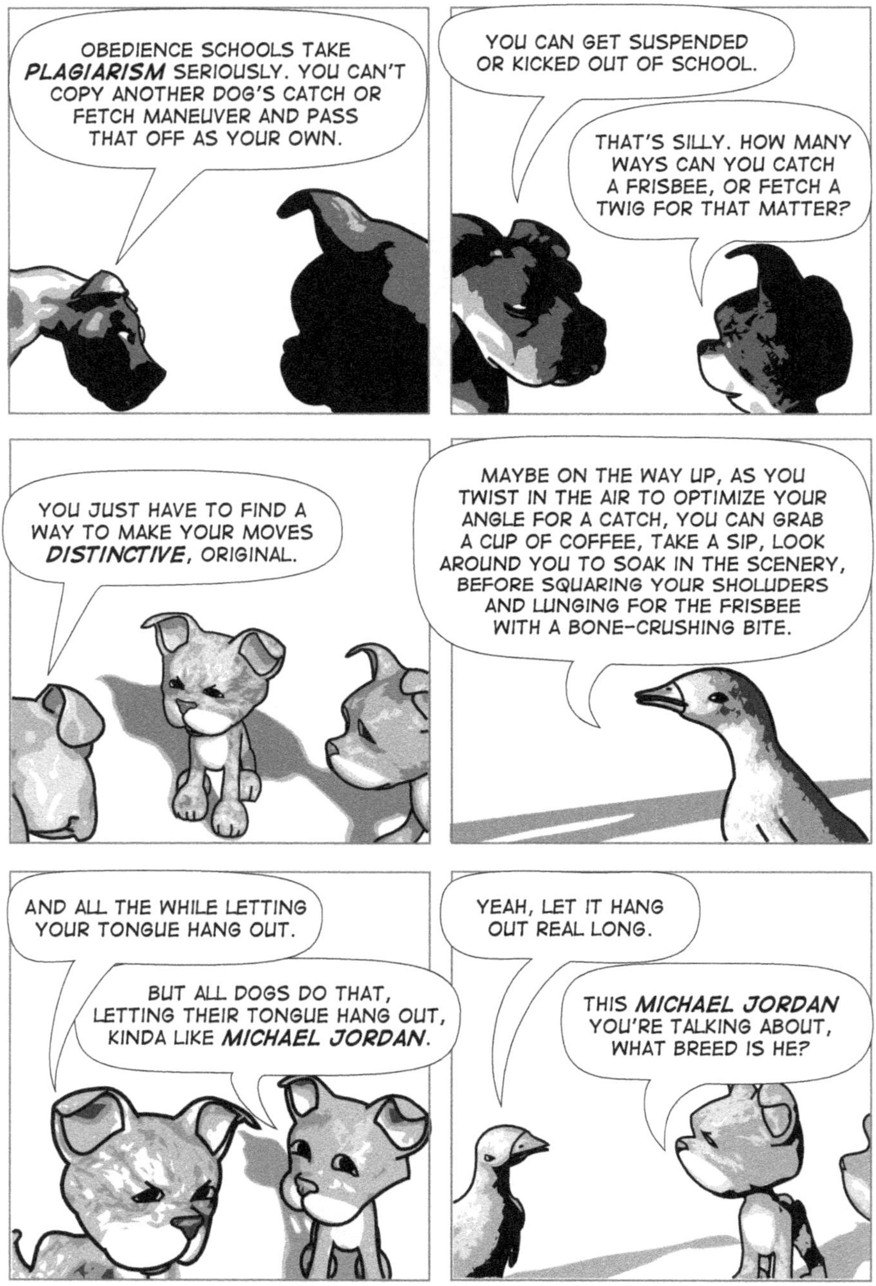
OBEDIENCE SCHOOLS TAKE PLAGIARISM SERIOUSLY. YOU CAN'T COPY ANOTHER DOG'S CATCH OR FETCH MANEUVER AND PASS THAT OFF AS YOUR OWN.
YOU CAN GET SUSPENDED OR KICKED OUT OF SCHOOL.
THAT'S SILLY. HOW MANY WAYS CAN YOU CATCH A FRISBEE, OR FETCH A TWIG FOR THAT MATTER?
YOU JUST HAVE TO FIND A WAY TO MAKE YOUR MOVES DISTINCTIVE, ORIGINAL.
MAYBE ON THE WAY UP, AS YOU TWIST IN THE AIR TO OPTIMIZE YOUR ANGLE FOR A CATCH, YOU CAN GRAB A CUP OF COFFEE, TAKE A SIP, LOOK AROUND YOU TO SOAK IN THE SCENERY, BEFORE SQUARING YOUR SHOLUDERS AND LUNGING FOR THE FRISBEE WITH A BONE-CRUSHING BITE.
AND ALL THE WHILE LETTING YOUR TONGUE HANG OUT.
BUT ALL DOGS DO THAT, LETTING THEIR TONGUE HANG OUT, KINDA LIKE MICHAEL JORDAN.
YEAH, LET IT HANG OUT REAL LONG.
THIS MICHAEL JORDAN YOU'RE TALKING ABOUT, WHAT BREED IS HE?

Homework

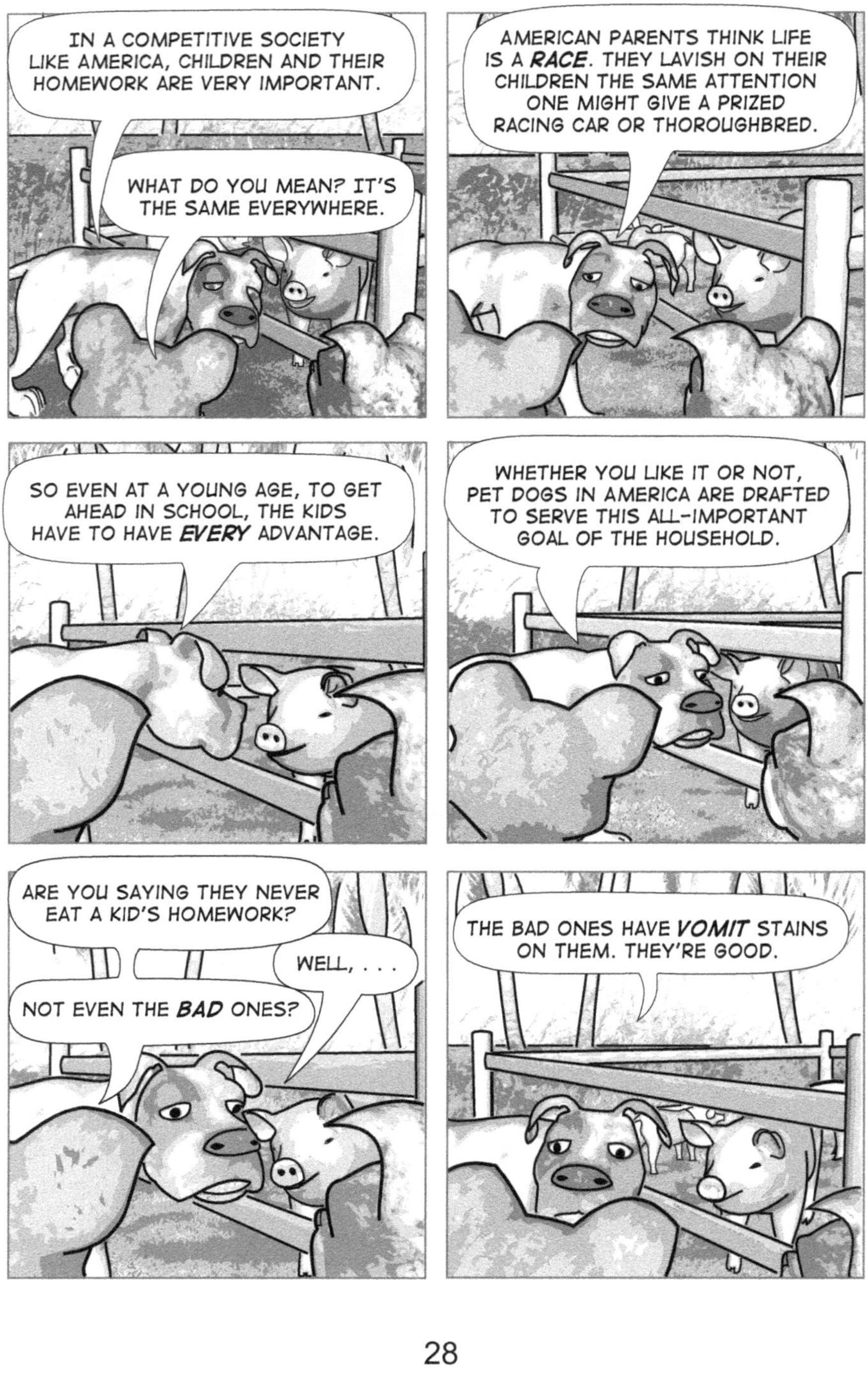
IN A COMPETITIVE SOCIETY LIKE AMERICA, CHILDREN AND THEIR HOMEWORK ARE VERY IMPORTANT.
WHAT DO YOU MEAN? IT'S THE SAME EVERYWHERE.
AMERICAN PARENTS THINK LIFE IS A *RACE*. THEY LAVISH ON THEIR CHILDREN THE SAME ATTENTION ONE MIGHT GIVE A PRIZED RACING CAR OR THOROUGHBRED.
SO EVEN AT A YOUNG AGE, TO GET AHEAD IN SCHOOL, THE KIDS HAVE TO HAVE *EVERY* ADVANTAGE.
WHETHER YOU LIKE IT OR NOT, PET DOGS IN AMERICA ARE DRAFTED TO SERVE THIS ALL-IMPORTANT GOAL OF THE HOUSEHOLD.
ARE YOU SAYING THEY NEVER EAT A KID'S HOMEWORK?
NOT EVEN THE *BAD* ONES?
WELL, . . .
THE BAD ONES HAVE *VOMIT* STAINS ON THEM. THEY'RE GOOD.

AN ARGUMENT IN THE HOUSEHOLD COULD BREAK OUT OVER HOMEWORK. THE HUMAN MOTHER MIGHT WANT THE KID'S DAD TO HELP OUT BUT NOT TOO MUCH AS TO DESTROY SELF-RELIANCE.

DAD ON THE OTHER HAND MIGHT INSIST ON GIVING ALL-OUT HELP WITH THE ASSIGNMENT.

WHY WOULD HE INSIST?

MAYBE BECAUSE THE DAD WANTS TO MAKE SURE THE HOMEWORK IS DONE RIGHT — THAT HE DOESN'T REPEAT THE SAME *STUPID* MISTAKES HIS *OWN* FATHER MADE HELPING HIM BACK THEN.

AH, THE SINS OF THE FATHER.

NAH, THAT'S THE SIN OF THE TEACHER. SHOULD HAVE *CHANGED* THE TEXTBOOK.

Cognitive and Other Tests

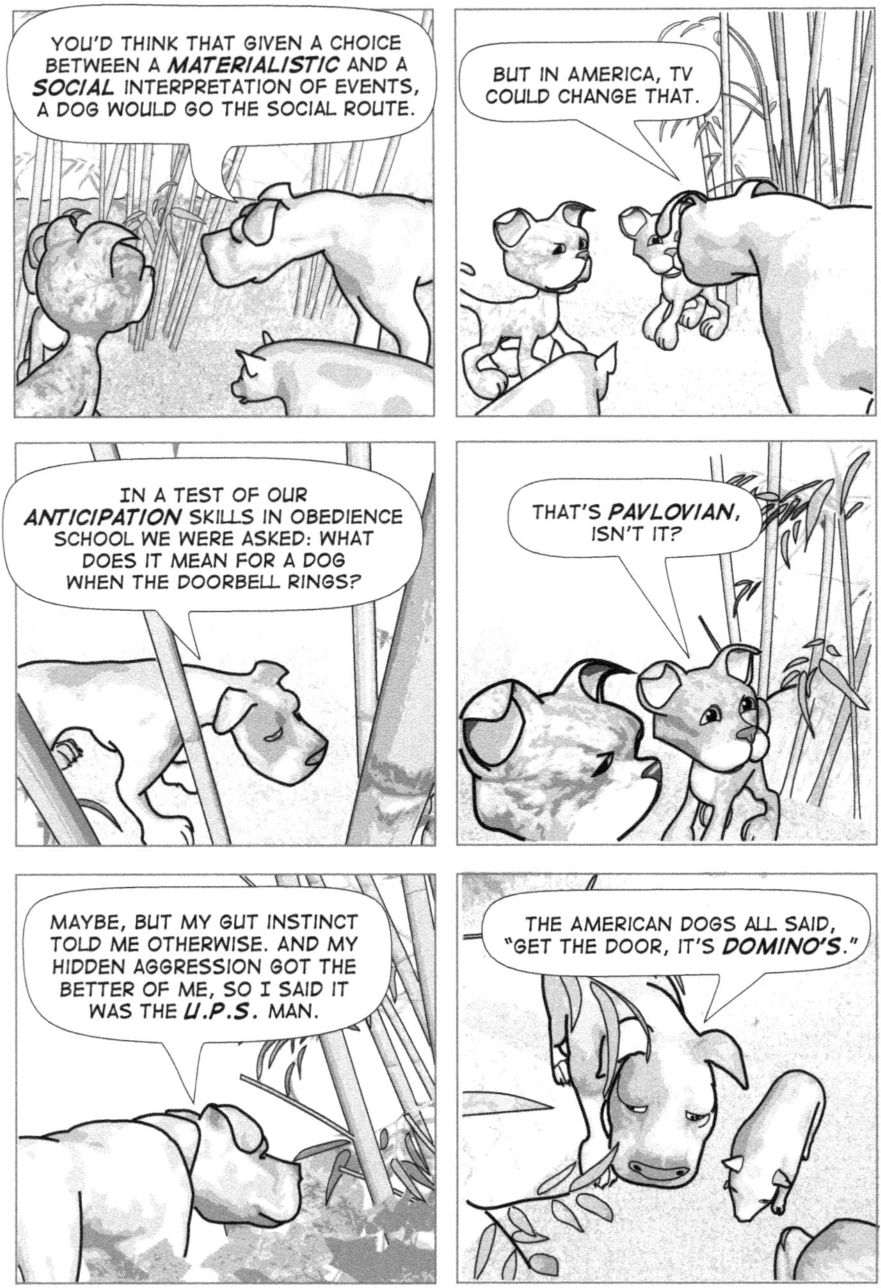
YOU'D THINK THAT GIVEN A CHOICE BETWEEN A MATERIALISTIC AND A SOCIAL INTERPRETATION OF EVENTS, A DOG WOULD GO THE SOCIAL ROUTE.
BUT IN AMERICA, TV COULD CHANGE THAT.
IN A TEST OF OUR ANTICIPATION SKILLS IN OBEDIENCE SCHOOL WE WERE ASKED: WHAT DOES IT MEAN FOR A DOG WHEN THE DOORBELL RINGS?
THAT'S PAVLOVIAN, ISN'T IT?
MAYBE, BUT MY GUT INSTINCT TOLD ME OTHERWISE. AND MY HIDDEN AGGRESSION GOT THE BETTER OF ME, SO I SAID IT WAS THE U.P.S. MAN.
THE AMERICAN DOGS ALL SAID, "GET THE DOOR, IT'S DOMINO'S."

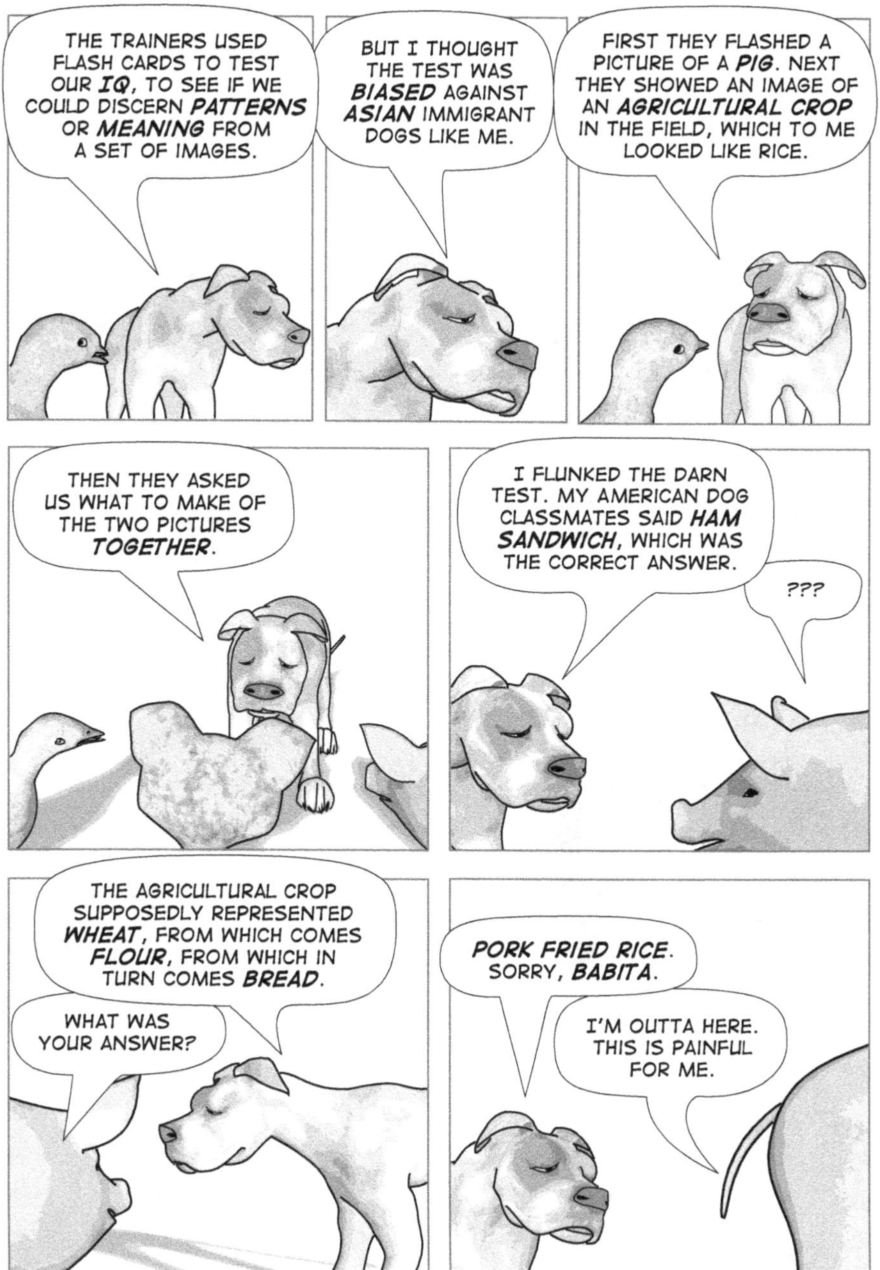

THE TRAINERS USED FLASH CARDS TO TEST OUR ***IQ***, TO SEE IF WE COULD DISCERN ***PATTERNS*** OR ***MEANING*** FROM A SET OF IMAGES.
BUT I THOUGHT THE TEST WAS ***BIASED*** AGAINST ***ASIAN*** IMMIGRANT DOGS LIKE ME.
FIRST THEY FLASHED A PICTURE OF A ***PIG***. NEXT THEY SHOWED AN IMAGE OF AN ***AGRICULTURAL CROP*** IN THE FIELD, WHICH TO ME LOOKED LIKE RICE.
THEN THEY ASKED US WHAT TO MAKE OF THE TWO PICTURES ***TOGETHER***.
I FLUNKED THE DARN TEST. MY AMERICAN DOG CLASSMATES SAID ***HAM SANDWICH***, WHICH WAS THE CORRECT ANSWER.
???
THE AGRICULTURAL CROP SUPPOSEDLY REPRESENTED ***WHEAT***, FROM WHICH COMES ***FLOUR***, FROM WHICH IN TURN COMES ***BREAD***.
WHAT WAS YOUR ANSWER?
PORK FRIED RICE. SORRY, ***BABITA***.
I'M OUTTA HERE. THIS IS PAINFUL FOR ME.

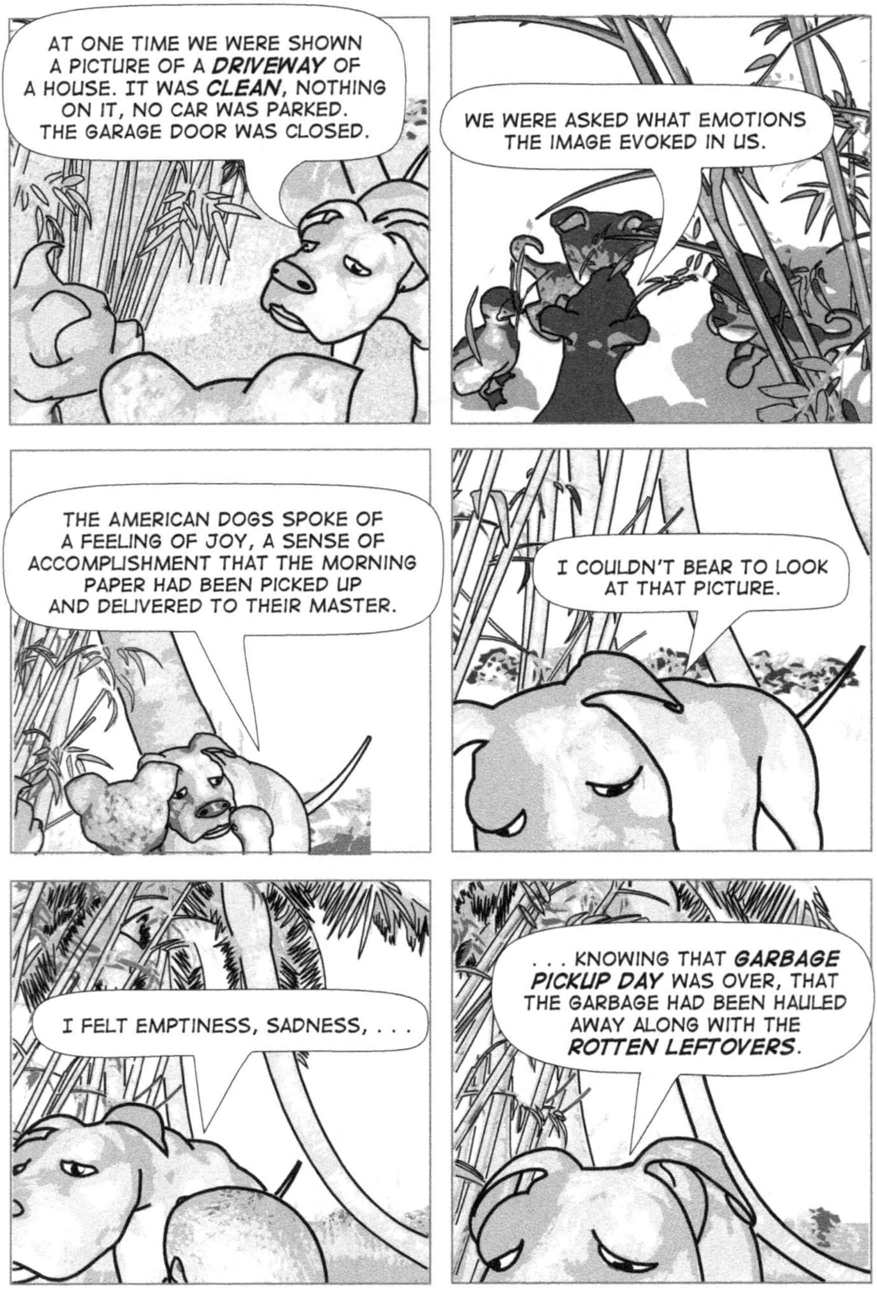
AT ONE TIME WE WERE SHOWN A PICTURE OF A DRIVEWAY OF A HOUSE. IT WAS CLEAN, NOTHING ON IT, NO CAR WAS PARKED. THE GARAGE DOOR WAS CLOSED.
WE WERE ASKED WHAT EMOTIONS THE IMAGE EVOKED IN US.
THE AMERICAN DOGS SPOKE OF A FEELING OF JOY, A SENSE OF ACCOMPLISHMENT THAT THE MORNING PAPER HAD BEEN PICKED UP AND DELIVERED TO THEIR MASTER.
I COULDN'T BEAR TO LOOK AT THAT PICTURE.
I FELT EMPTINESS, SADNESS, . . .
. . . KNOWING THAT GARBAGE PICKUP DAY WAS OVER, THAT THE GARBAGE HAD BEEN HAULED AWAY ALONG WITH THE ROTTEN LEFTOVERS.

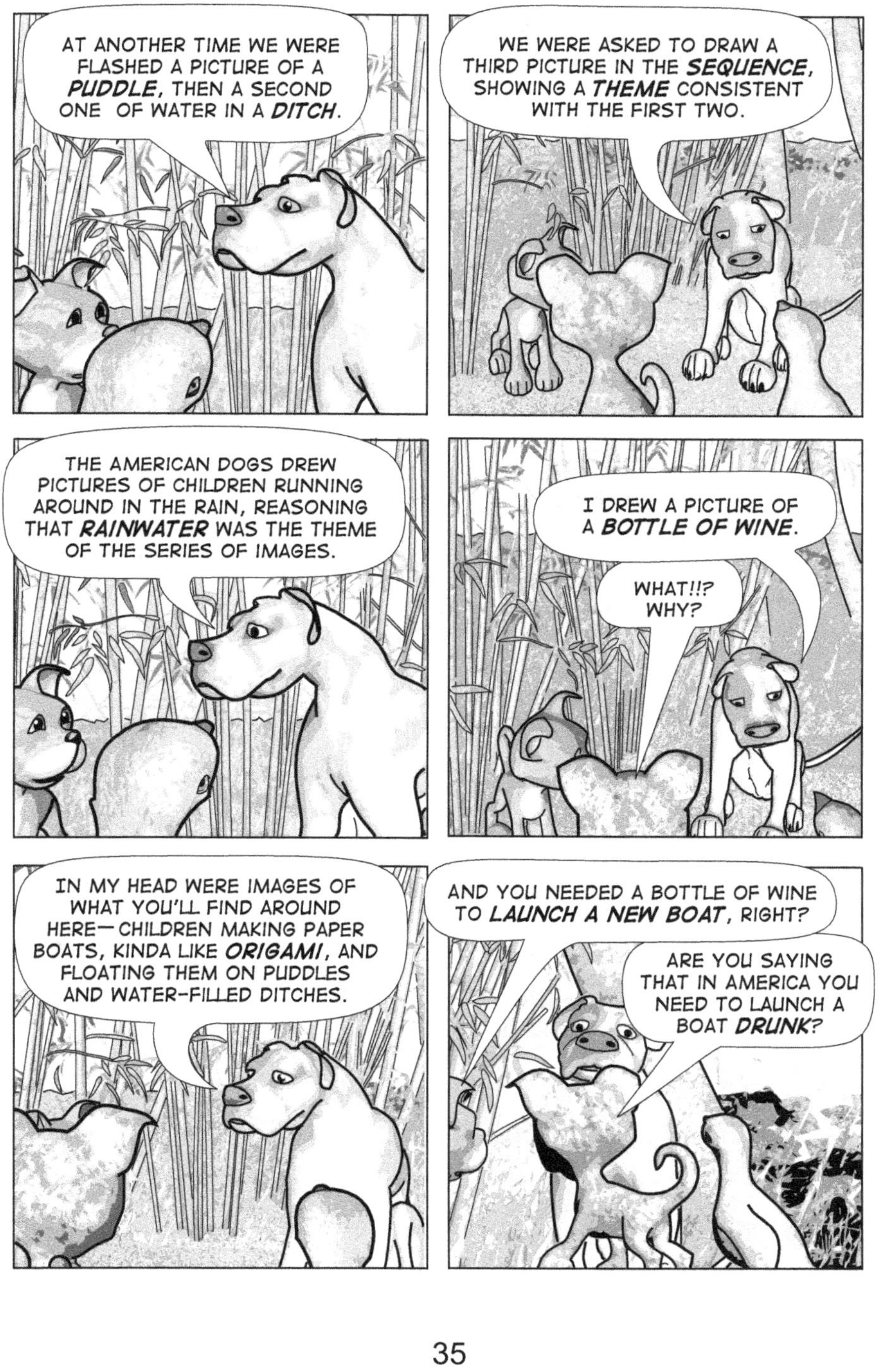
AT ANOTHER TIME WE WERE FLASHED A PICTURE OF A PUDDLE, THEN A SECOND ONE OF WATER IN A DITCH.
WE WERE ASKED TO DRAW A THIRD PICTURE IN THE SEQUENCE, SHOWING A THEME CONSISTENT WITH THE FIRST TWO.
THE AMERICAN DOGS DREW PICTURES OF CHILDREN RUNNING AROUND IN THE RAIN, REASONING THAT RAINWATER WAS THE THEME OF THE SERIES OF IMAGES.
I DREW A PICTURE OF A BOTTLE OF WINE.
WHAT!!? WHY?
IN MY HEAD WERE IMAGES OF WHAT YOU'LL FIND AROUND HERE—CHILDREN MAKING PAPER BOATS, KINDA LIKE ORIGAMI, AND FLOATING THEM ON PUDDLES AND WATER-FILLED DITCHES.
AND YOU NEEDED A BOTTLE OF WINE TO LAUNCH A NEW BOAT, RIGHT?
ARE YOU SAYING THAT IN AMERICA YOU NEED TO LAUNCH A BOAT DRUNK?

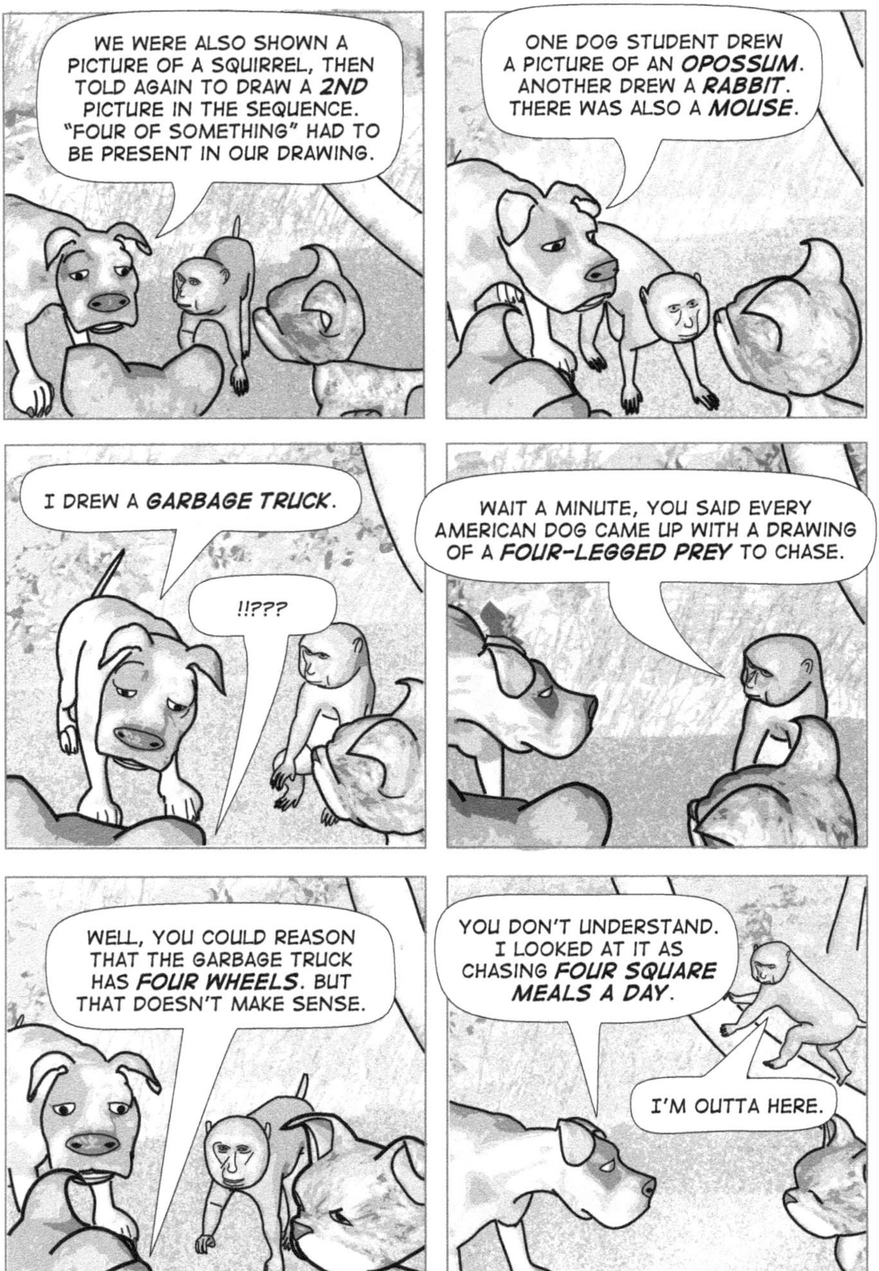

WE WERE ALSO SHOWN A PICTURE OF A SQUIRREL, THEN TOLD AGAIN TO DRAW A 2ND PICTURE IN THE SEQUENCE. "FOUR OF SOMETHING" HAD TO BE PRESENT IN OUR DRAWING.
ONE DOG STUDENT DREW A PICTURE OF AN OPOSSUM. ANOTHER DREW A RABBIT. THERE WAS ALSO A MOUSE.
I DREW A GARBAGE TRUCK.
!!???
WAIT A MINUTE, YOU SAID EVERY AMERICAN DOG CAME UP WITH A DRAWING OF A FOUR-LEGGED PREY TO CHASE.
WELL, YOU COULD REASON THAT THE GARBAGE TRUCK HAS FOUR WHEELS. BUT THAT DOESN'T MAKE SENSE.
YOU DON'T UNDERSTAND. I LOOKED AT IT AS CHASING FOUR SQUARE MEALS A DAY.
I'M OUTTA HERE.

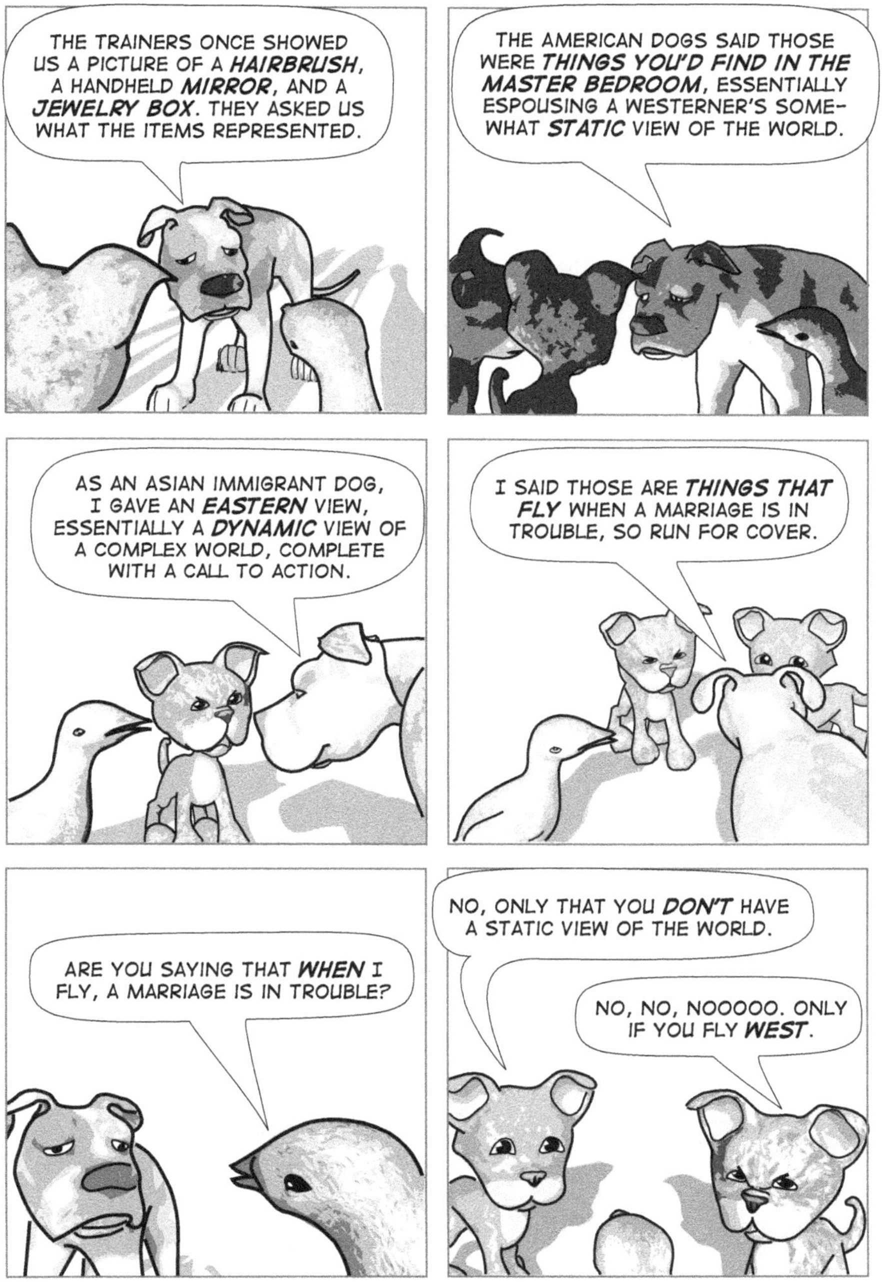
THE TRAINERS ONCE SHOWED US A PICTURE OF A HAIRBRUSH, A HANDHELD MIRROR, AND A JEWELRY BOX. THEY ASKED US WHAT THE ITEMS REPRESENTED.
THE AMERICAN DOGS SAID THOSE WERE THINGS YOU'D FIND IN THE MASTER BEDROOM, ESSENTIALLY ESPOUSING A WESTERNER'S SOME-WHAT STATIC VIEW OF THE WORLD.
AS AN ASIAN IMMIGRANT DOG, I GAVE AN EASTERN VIEW, ESSENTIALLY A DYNAMIC VIEW OF A COMPLEX WORLD, COMPLETE WITH A CALL TO ACTION.
I SAID THOSE ARE THINGS THAT FLY WHEN A MARRIAGE IS IN TROUBLE, SO RUN FOR COVER.
ARE YOU SAYING THAT WHEN I FLY, A MARRIAGE IS IN TROUBLE?
NO, ONLY THAT YOU DON'T HAVE A STATIC VIEW OF THE WORLD.
NO, NO, NOOOOO. ONLY IF YOU FLY WEST.

Household Decisions

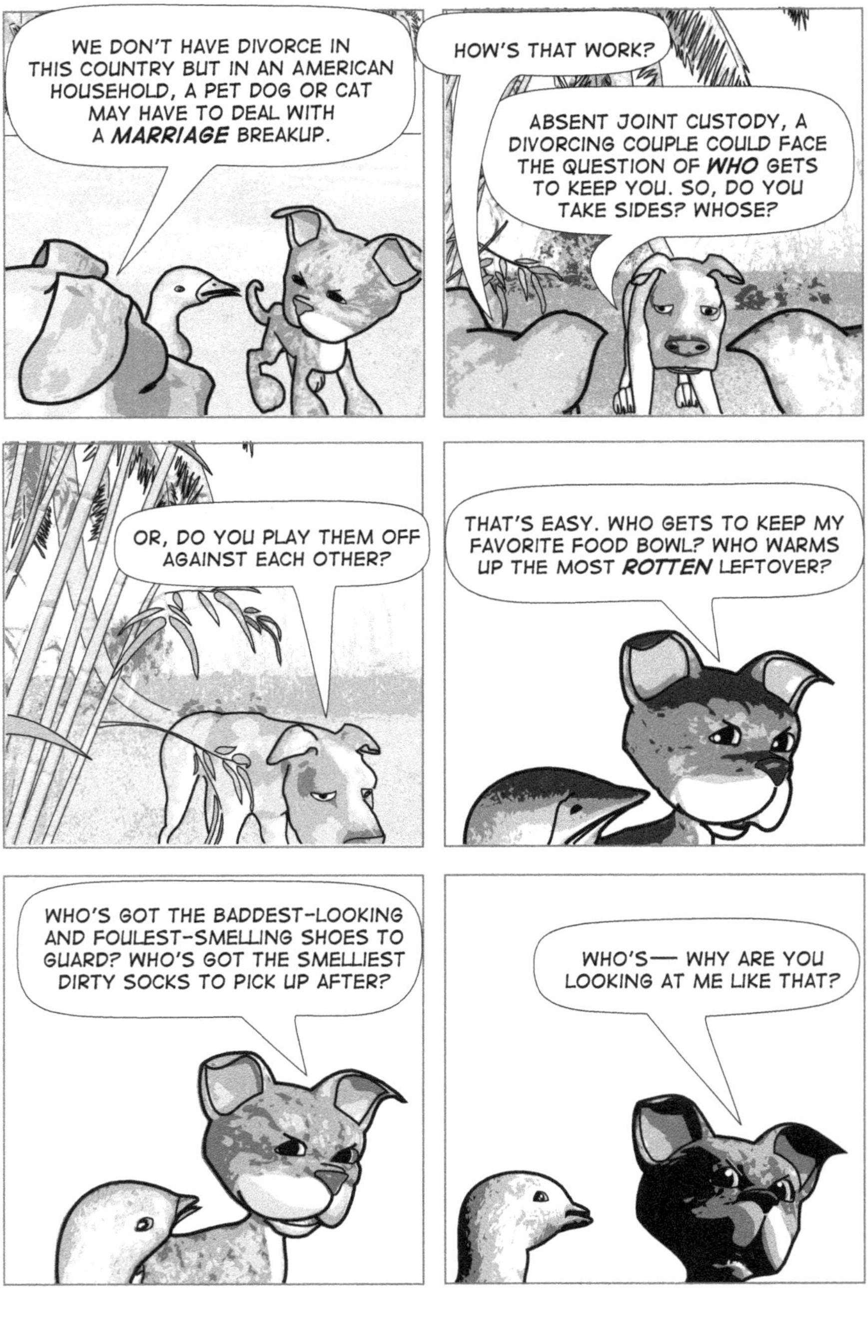
WE DON'T HAVE DIVORCE IN THIS COUNTRY BUT IN AN AMERICAN HOUSEHOLD, A PET DOG OR CAT MAY HAVE TO DEAL WITH A *MARRIAGE* BREAKUP.
HOW'S THAT WORK?
ABSENT JOINT CUSTODY, A DIVORCING COUPLE COULD FACE THE QUESTION OF *WHO* GETS TO KEEP YOU. SO, DO YOU TAKE SIDES? WHOSE?
OR, DO YOU PLAY THEM OFF AGAINST EACH OTHER?
THAT'S EASY. WHO GETS TO KEEP MY FAVORITE FOOD BOWL? WHO WARMS UP THE MOST *ROTTEN* LEFTOVER?
WHO'S GOT THE BADDEST-LOOKING AND FOULEST-SMELLING SHOES TO GUARD? WHO'S GOT THE SMELLIEST DIRTY SOCKS TO PICK UP AFTER?
WHO'S— WHY ARE YOU LOOKING AT ME LIKE THAT?

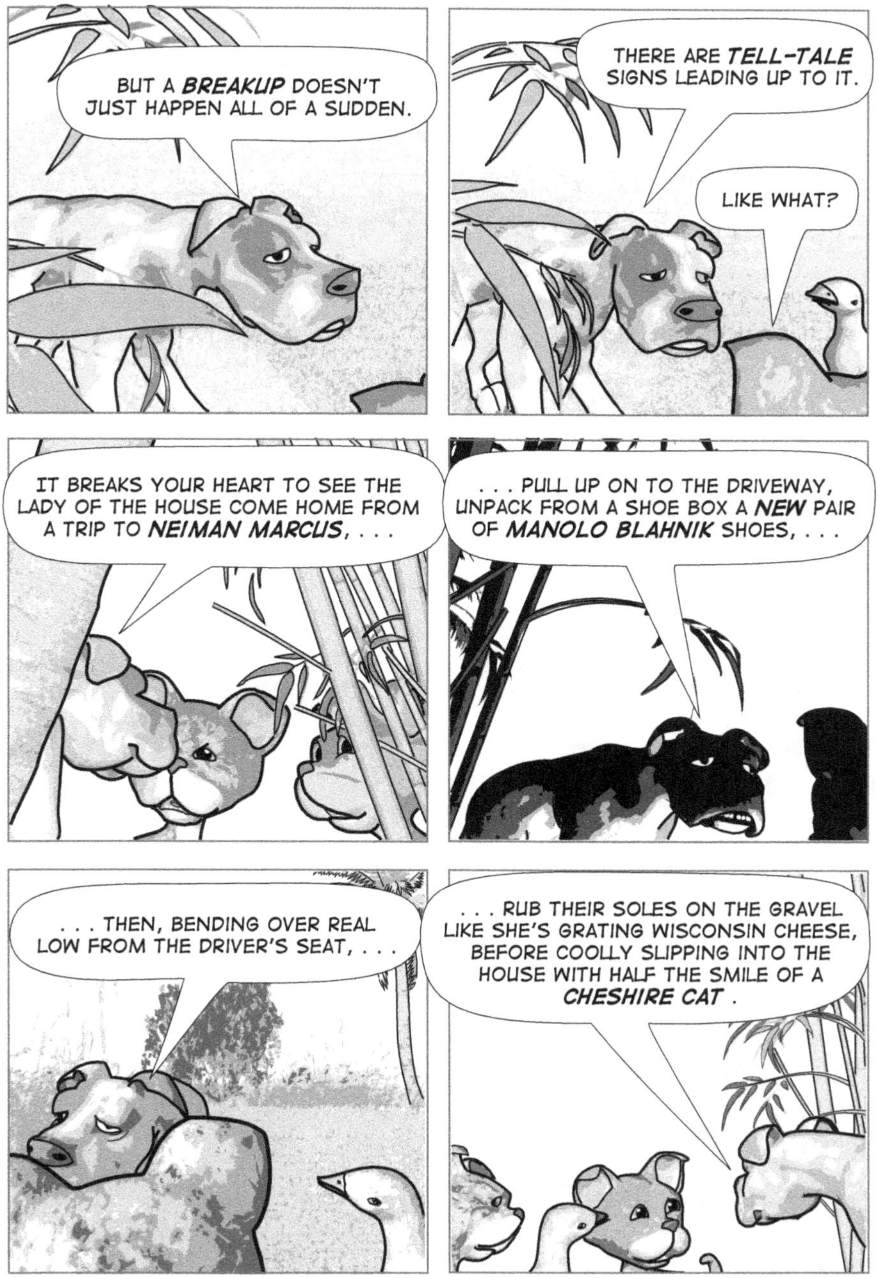
BUT A BREAKUP DOESN'T JUST HAPPEN ALL OF A SUDDEN.
THERE ARE TELL-TALE SIGNS LEADING UP TO IT.
LIKE WHAT?
IT BREAKS YOUR HEART TO SEE THE LADY OF THE HOUSE COME HOME FROM A TRIP TO NEIMAN MARCUS, . . .
. . . PULL UP ON TO THE DRIVEWAY, UNPACK FROM A SHOE BOX A NEW PAIR OF MANOLO BLAHNIK SHOES, . . .
. . . THEN, BENDING OVER REAL LOW FROM THE DRIVER'S SEAT, . . .
. . . RUB THEIR SOLES ON THE GRAVEL LIKE SHE'S GRATING WISCONSIN CHEESE, BEFORE COOLLY SLIPPING INTO THE HOUSE WITH HALF THE SMILE OF A CHESHIRE CAT .

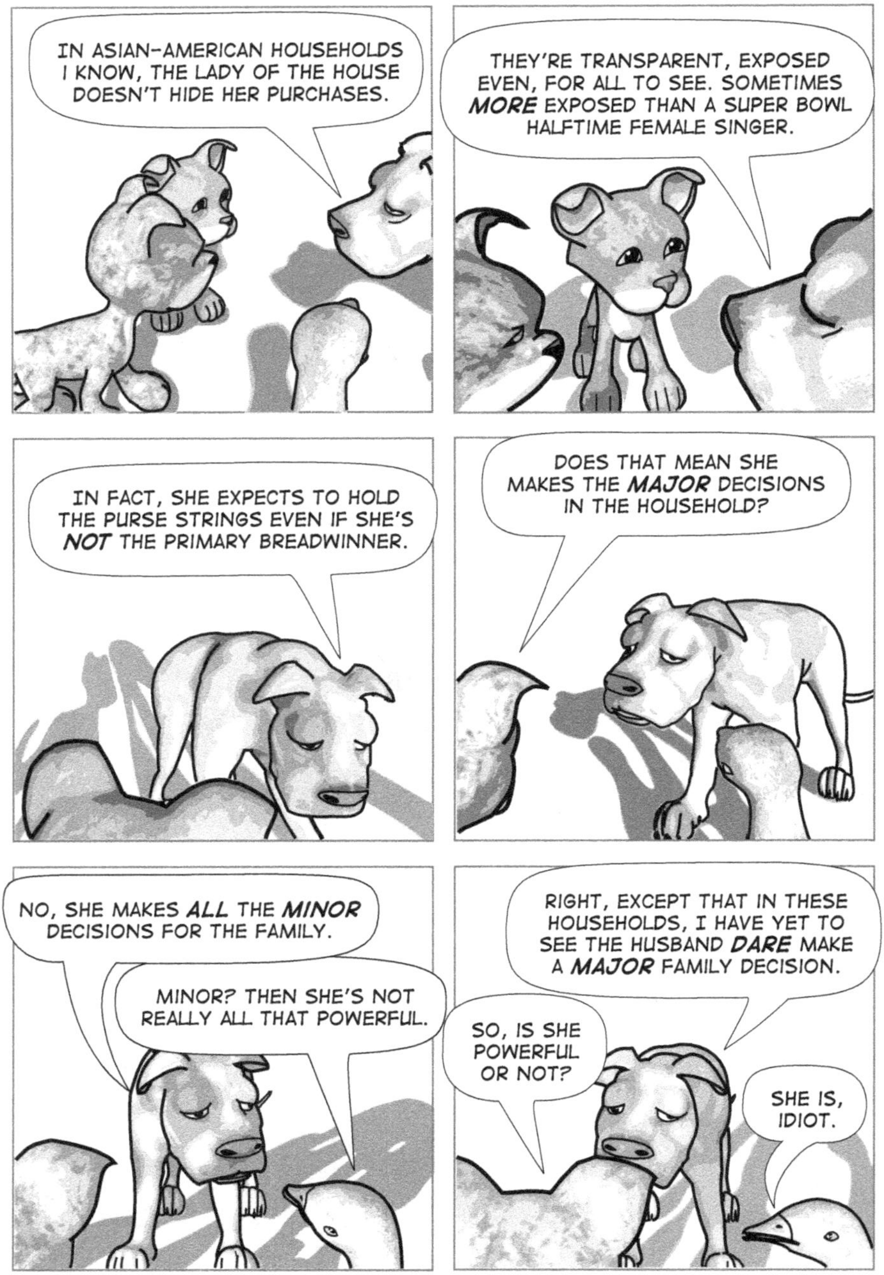
IN ASIAN-AMERICAN HOUSEHOLDS I KNOW, THE LADY OF THE HOUSE DOESN'T HIDE HER PURCHASES.
THEY'RE TRANSPARENT, EXPOSED EVEN, FOR ALL TO SEE. SOMETIMES *MORE* EXPOSED THAN A SUPER BOWL HALFTIME FEMALE SINGER.
IN FACT, SHE EXPECTS TO HOLD THE PURSE STRINGS EVEN IF SHE'S *NOT* THE PRIMARY BREADWINNER.
DOES THAT MEAN SHE MAKES THE *MAJOR* DECISIONS IN THE HOUSEHOLD?
NO, SHE MAKES *ALL* THE *MINOR* DECISIONS FOR THE FAMILY.
MINOR? THEN SHE'S NOT REALLY ALL THAT POWERFUL.
RIGHT, EXCEPT THAT IN THESE HOUSEHOLDS, I HAVE YET TO SEE THE HUSBAND *DARE* MAKE A *MAJOR* FAMILY DECISION.
SO, IS SHE POWERFUL OR NOT?
SHE IS, IDIOT.

Study Abroad Program

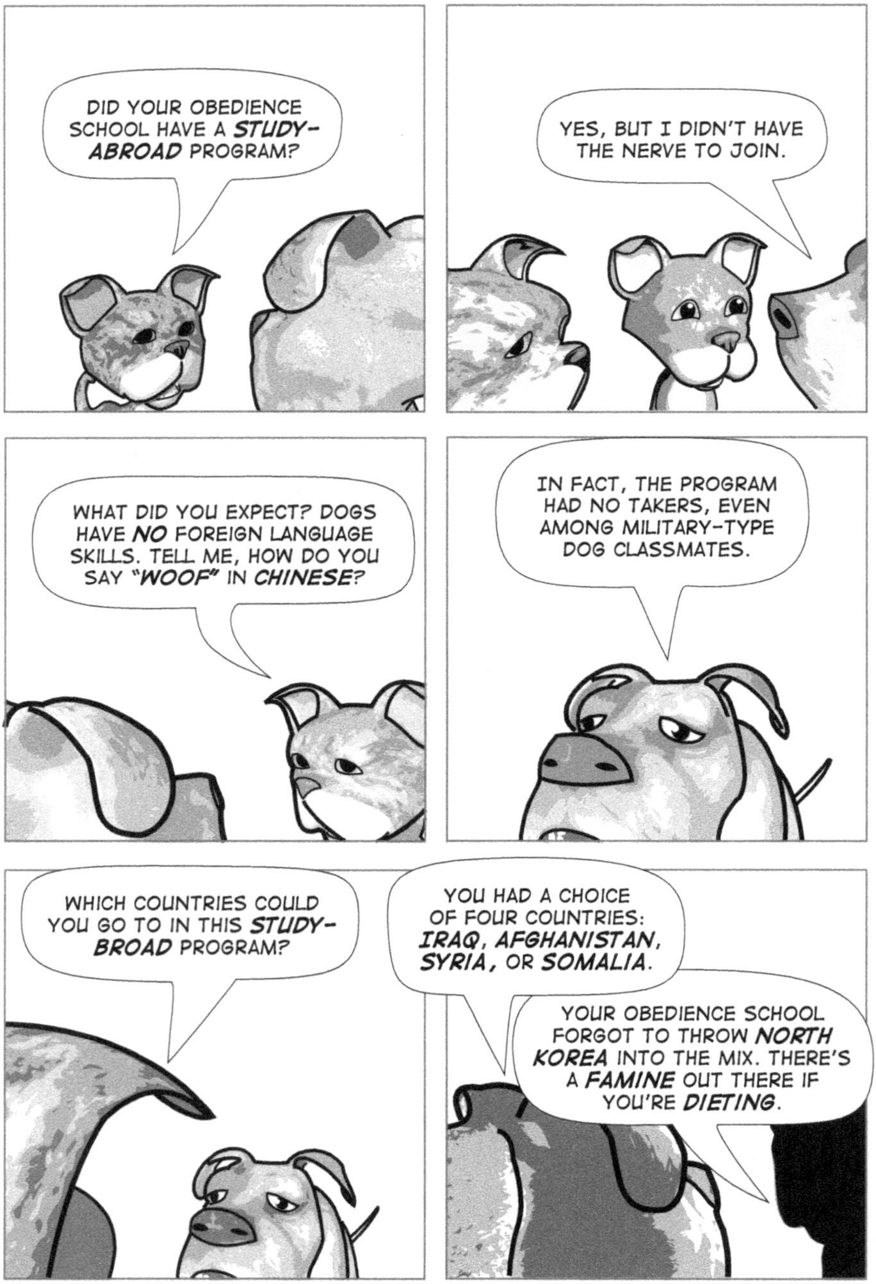
DID YOUR OBEDIENCE SCHOOL HAVE A STUDY-ABROAD PROGRAM?
YES, BUT I DIDN'T HAVE THE NERVE TO JOIN.
WHAT DID YOU EXPECT? DOGS HAVE NO FOREIGN LANGUAGE SKILLS. TELL ME, HOW DO YOU SAY "WOOF" IN CHINESE?
IN FACT, THE PROGRAM HAD NO TAKERS, EVEN AMONG MILITARY-TYPE DOG CLASSMATES.
WHICH COUNTRIES COULD YOU GO TO IN THIS STUDY-BROAD PROGRAM?
YOU HAD A CHOICE OF FOUR COUNTRIES: IRAQ, AFGHANISTAN, SYRIA, OR SOMALIA.
YOUR OBEDIENCE SCHOOL FORGOT TO THROW NORTH KOREA INTO THE MIX. THERE'S A FAMINE OUT THERE IF YOU'RE DIETING.

The Charms of America

45

IT IS EASY FOR AN IMMIGRANT DOG TO FALL FOR THE CHARMS OF AMERICA, OF A NEW CULTURE IN WHICH THERE SEEMS TO BE SO MUCH OF EVERYTHING.
HERE, YOU CAN'T THINK OF CHASING A COVERTED JEEP LIKE THE PASSENGER JEEPNEY THAT WE HAVE, MUCH LESS A PEDICAB, UNTIL YOU KNOW WHERE YOUR NEXT MEAL IS COMING FROM.
BUT IN AMERICA, YOU GOT TIME, CHOICES. YOU CHASE CARS, SUVS.
DO YOU REALLY HAVE TO CHASE AN OUTSIZE CAR?
YOU'RE NOT JUST CHASING AN OUTSIZE CAR, YOU'RE CHASING AN OUTSIZE LIFESTYLE.
AND OUTSIZE FUMES.

ARE FIRE HYDRANTS IN AMERICA BIG OR SMALL?
I'M IN MY BEST ELEMENT WHEN I CAN TOWER OVER A FIRE HYDRANT. BUT MORE THAN A MATTER OF ELEVATION, IT'S A MATTER OF PROPORTION.
SO THERE'S HOPE FOR A *SHORT* DOG LIKE ME.
THERE IS. ***HIGH HEELS, PLATFORM BOOTS, ROUND TOES, HIGH-DEFINITION COLOR,*** YOU NAME IT. AMERICA HAS ***EVERYTHING***.
COLOR? ARE YOU SAYING I WILL BE ABLE TO SEE ***IN*** COLOR IN AMERICA? AND IN ***HD***?

IN THE SPIRIT OF THE HOLIDAY SEASON, IT IS CUSTOMARY FOR HUMANS IN AMERICA TO TIP, SAY, THE APARTMENT BUILDING DOORMAN . . .
. . . THE NEWSPAPER DELIVERY BOY, THE CAB DRIVER, THE GARBAGE COLLECTOR, . . .
THE GARBAGE COLLECTOR? IF IT WERE ME, I WOULDN'T BOTHER. I WILL TIP EVERYONE EXCEPT THE GARBAGE COLLECTOR.
WHY IS THAT?
GOODNESS. WHAT DO YOU GIVE A HUMAN WHO HAS EVERYTHING?
NOT EVEN A ROCH-HARD FRUIT CAKE, EH?

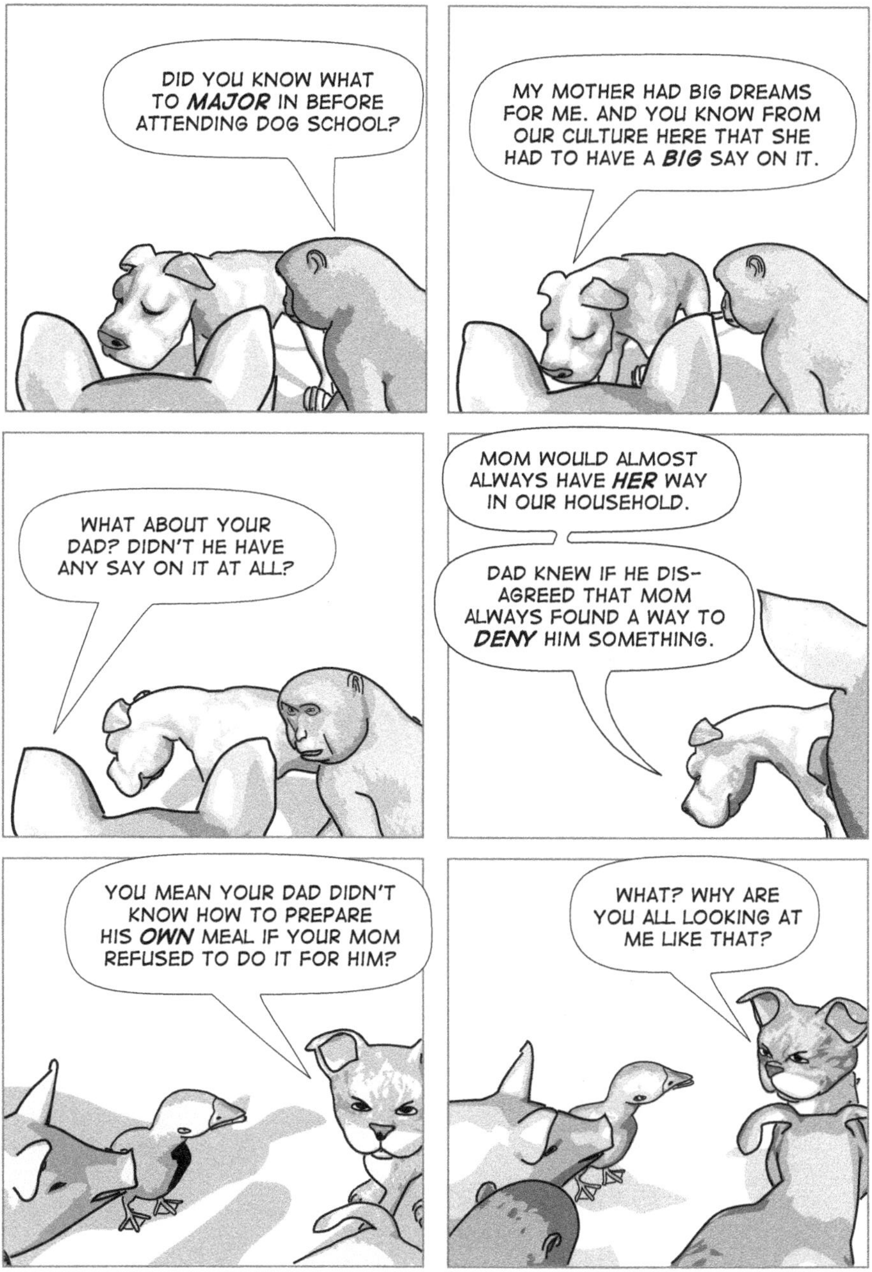
DID YOU KNOW WHAT TO MAJOR IN BEFORE ATTENDING DOG SCHOOL?
MY MOTHER HAD BIG DREAMS FOR ME. AND YOU KNOW FROM OUR CULTURE HERE THAT SHE HAD TO HAVE A BIG SAY ON IT.
WHAT ABOUT YOUR DAD? DIDN'T HE HAVE ANY SAY ON IT AT ALL?
MOM WOULD ALMOST ALWAYS HAVE HER WAY IN OUR HOUSEHOLD.
DAD KNEW IF HE DIS-AGREED THAT MOM ALWAYS FOUND A WAY TO DENY HIM SOMETHING.
YOU MEAN YOUR DAD DIDN'T KNOW HOW TO PREPARE HIS OWN MEAL IF YOUR MOM REFUSED TO DO IT FOR HIM?
WHAT? WHY ARE YOU ALL LOOKING AT ME LIKE THAT?

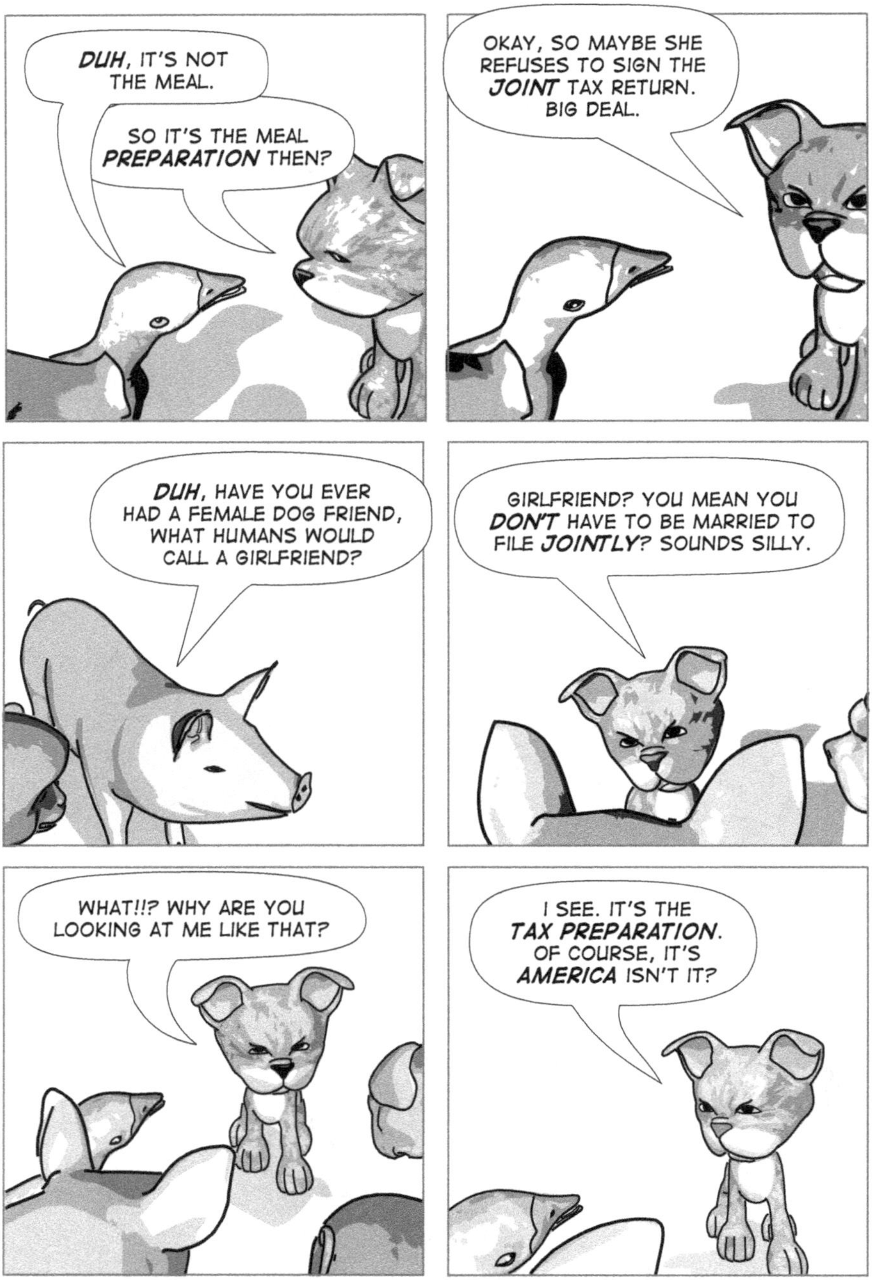
DUH, IT'S NOT THE MEAL.
SO IT'S THE MEAL PREPARATION THEN?
OKAY, SO MAYBE SHE REFUSES TO SIGN THE JOINT TAX RETURN. BIG DEAL.
DUH, HAVE YOU EVER HAD A FEMALE DOG FRIEND, WHAT HUMANS WOULD CALL A GIRLFRIEND?
GIRLFRIEND? YOU MEAN YOU DON'T HAVE TO BE MARRIED TO FILE JOINTLY? SOUNDS SILLY.
WHAT!!? WHY ARE YOU LOOKING AT ME LIKE THAT?
I SEE. IT'S THE TAX PREPARATION. OF COURSE, IT'S AMERICA ISN'T IT?

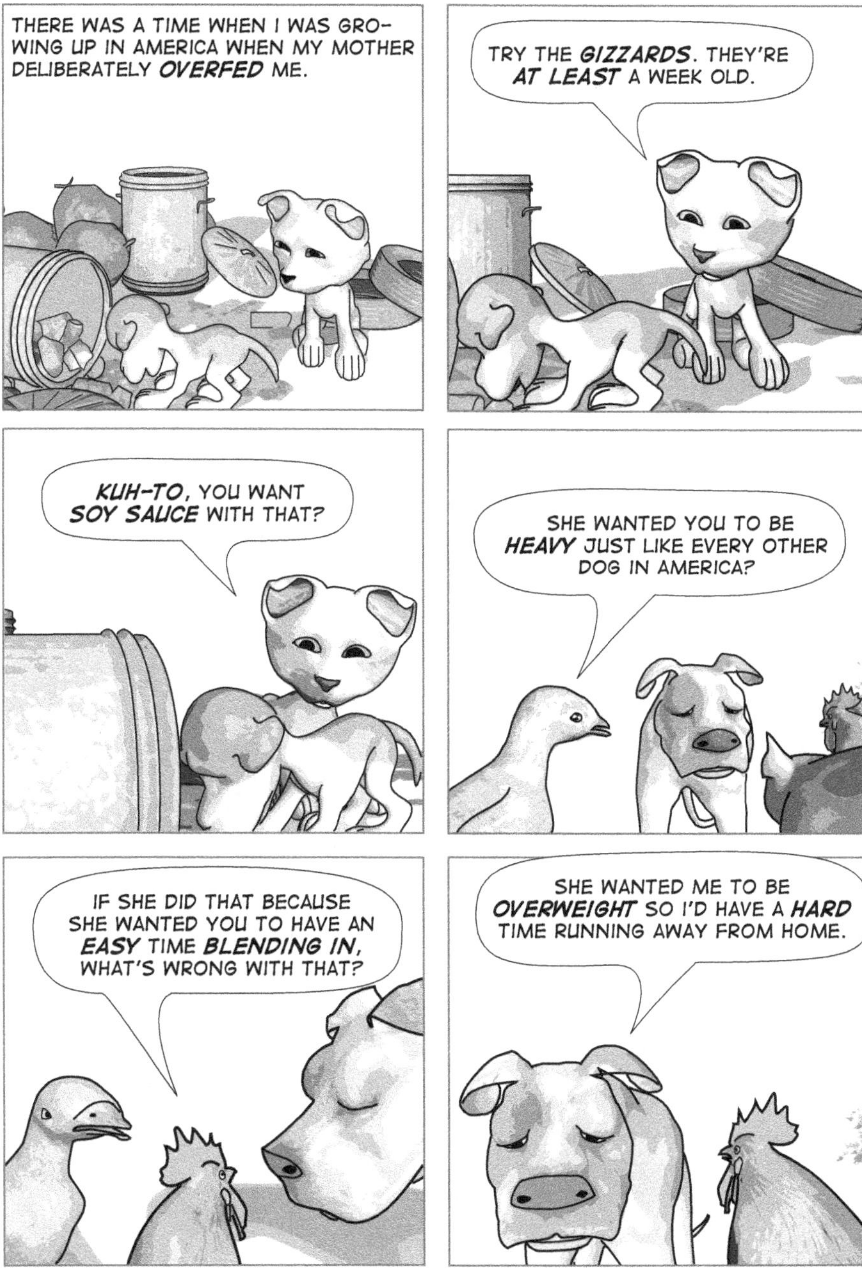
THERE WAS A TIME WHEN I WAS GROWING UP IN AMERICA WHEN MY MOTHER DELIBERATELY OVERFED ME.
TRY THE GIZZARDS. THEY'RE AT LEAST A WEEK OLD.
KUH-TO, YOU WANT SOY SAUCE WITH THAT?
SHE WANTED YOU TO BE HEAVY JUST LIKE EVERY OTHER DOG IN AMERICA?
IF SHE DID THAT BECAUSE SHE WANTED YOU TO HAVE AN EASY TIME BLENDING IN, WHAT'S WRONG WITH THAT?
SHE WANTED ME TO BE OVERWEIGHT SO I'D HAVE A HARD TIME RUNNING AWAY FROM HOME.

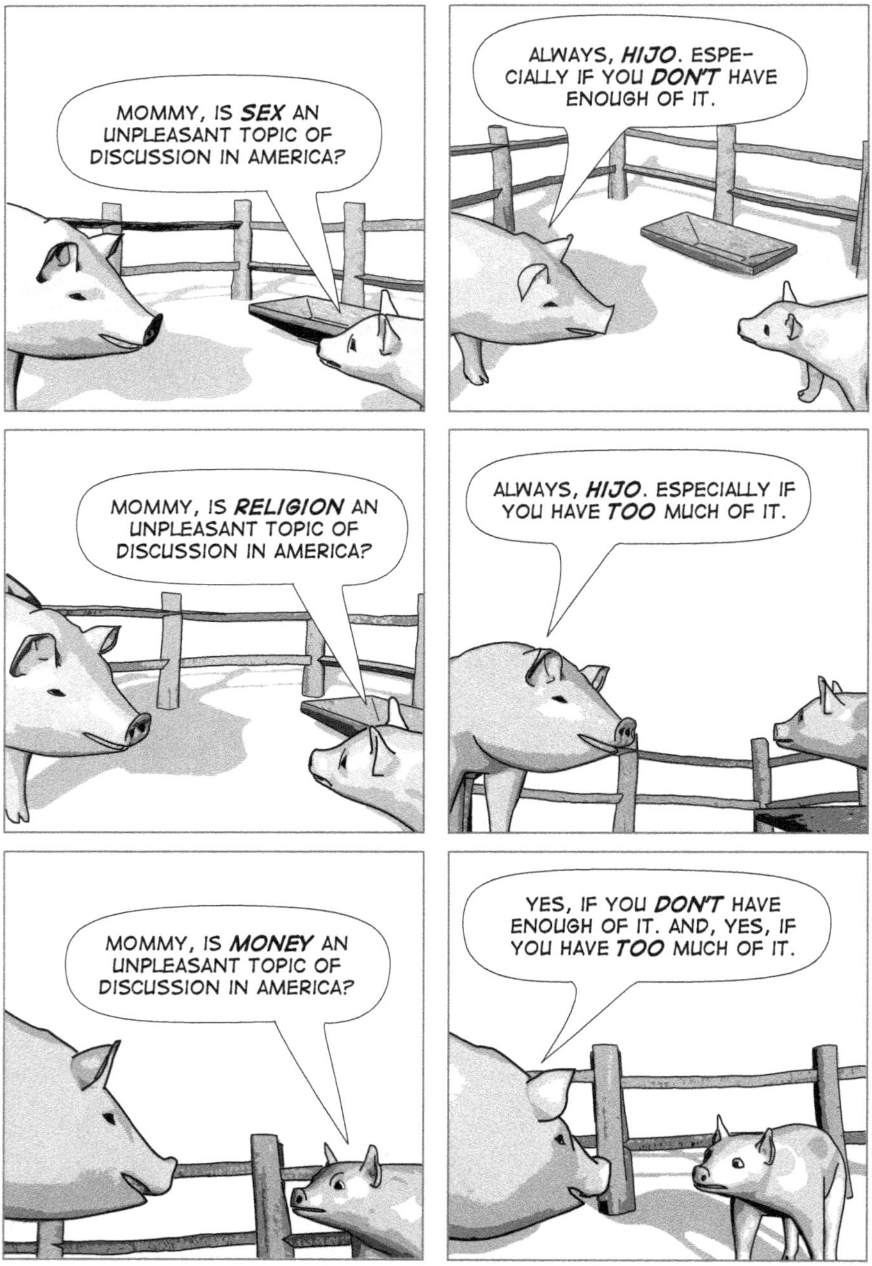
MOMMY, IS SEX AN UNPLEASANT TOPIC OF DISCUSSION IN AMERICA?
ALWAYS, HIJO. ESPE- CIALLY IF YOU DON'T HAVE ENOUGH OF IT.
MOMMY, IS RELIGION AN UNPLEASANT TOPIC OF DISCUSSION IN AMERICA?
ALWAYS, HIJO. ESPECIALLY IF YOU HAVE TOO MUCH OF IT.
MOMMY, IS MONEY AN UNPLEASANT TOPIC OF DISCUSSION IN AMERICA?
YES, IF YOU DON'T HAVE ENOUGH OF IT. AND, YES, IF YOU HAVE TOO MUCH OF IT.

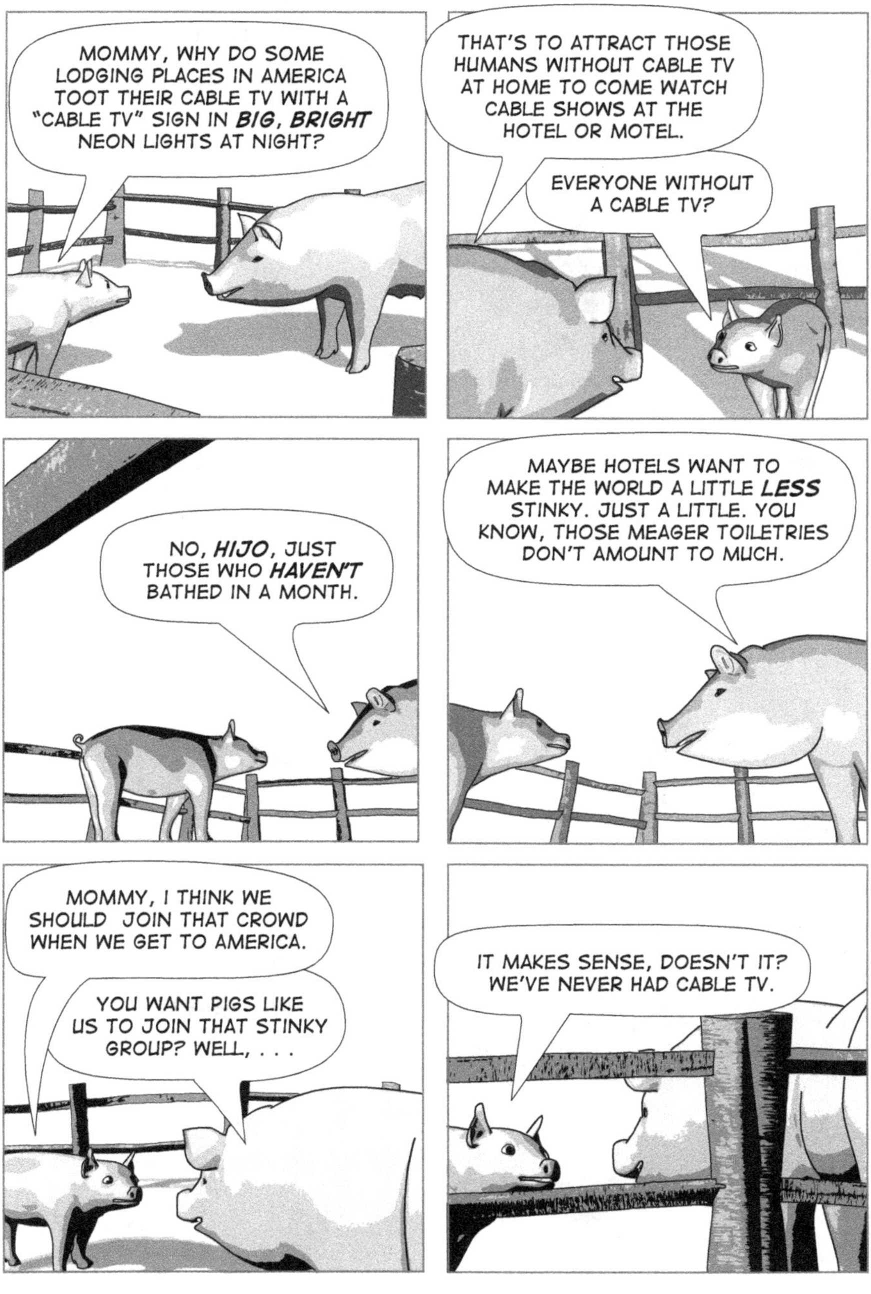
MOMMY, WHY DO SOME LODGING PLACES IN AMERICA TOOT THEIR CABLE TV WITH A "CABLE TV" SIGN IN BIG, BRIGHT NEON LIGHTS AT NIGHT?
THAT'S TO ATTRACT THOSE HUMANS WITHOUT CABLE TV AT HOME TO COME WATCH CABLE SHOWS AT THE HOTEL OR MOTEL.
EVERYONE WITHOUT A CABLE TV?
NO, HIJO, JUST THOSE WHO HAVEN'T BATHED IN A MONTH.
MAYBE HOTELS WANT TO MAKE THE WORLD A LITTLE LESS STINKY. JUST A LITTLE. YOU KNOW, THOSE MEAGER TOILETRIES DON'T AMOUNT TO MUCH.
MOMMY, I THINK WE SHOULD JOIN THAT CROWD WHEN WE GET TO AMERICA.
YOU WANT PIGS LIKE US TO JOIN THAT STINKY GROUP? WELL, . . .
IT MAKES SENSE, DOESN'T IT? WE'VE NEVER HAD CABLE TV.

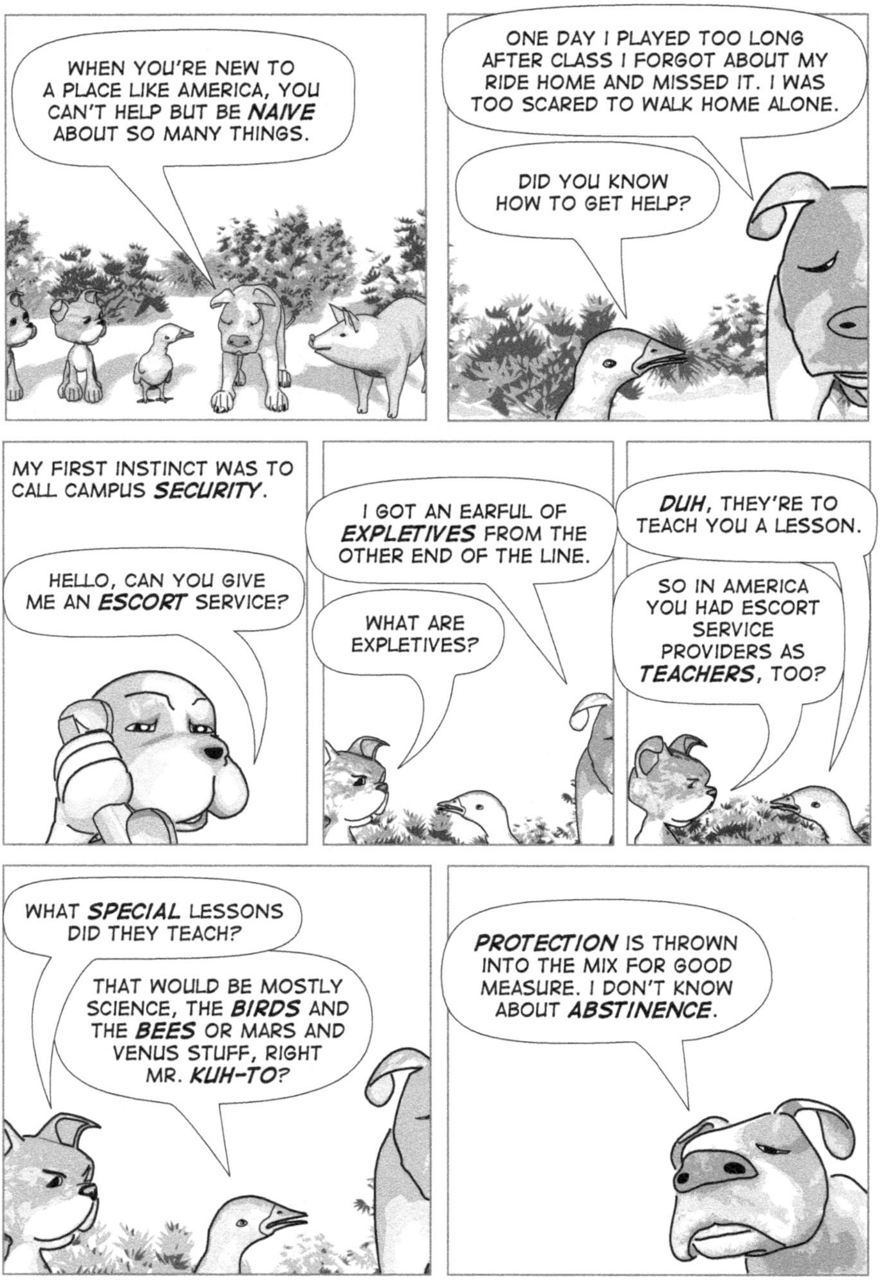
WHEN YOU'RE NEW TO A PLACE LIKE AMERICA, YOU CAN'T HELP BUT BE *NAIVE* ABOUT SO MANY THINGS.
ONE DAY I PLAYED TOO LONG AFTER CLASS I FORGOT ABOUT MY RIDE HOME AND MISSED IT. I WAS TOO SCARED TO WALK HOME ALONE.
DID YOU KNOW HOW TO GET HELP?
MY FIRST INSTINCT WAS TO CALL CAMPUS *SECURITY*.
HELLO, CAN YOU GIVE ME AN *ESCORT* SERVICE?
I GOT AN EARFUL OF *EXPLETIVES* FROM THE OTHER END OF THE LINE.
WHAT ARE EXPLETIVES?
DUH, THEY'RE TO TEACH YOU A LESSON.
SO IN AMERICA YOU HAD ESCORT SERVICE PROVIDERS AS *TEACHERS*, TOO?
WHAT *SPECIAL* LESSONS DID THEY TEACH?
THAT WOULD BE MOSTLY SCIENCE, THE *BIRDS* AND THE *BEES* OR MARS AND VENUS STUFF, RIGHT MR. *KUH-TO*?
PROTECTION IS THROWN INTO THE MIX FOR GOOD MEASURE. I DON'T KNOW ABOUT *ABSTINENCE*.

Grades and Report Cards

WHAT ABOUT YOUR REPORT CARD? WERE YOU EVER AFRAID YOUR MOM OR YOUR MASTER WOULD SEE YOUR POOR GRADES AND GO NUTS?
NO, NOT AT ALL. AMERICAN SOCIETY IS BIG ON PRIVACY, BORDERING ON ABSURDNESS.
IF YOU'RE A STUDENT OF AGE, YOU CAN HIDE YOUR GOOD AND BAD GRADES FROM EVEN THOSE WHO PAY FOR YOUR SCHOOLING.
WHAT, NO ACCOUNTABILITY? NO NEED FOR AN EXCUSE EVEN IF YOU HAVE MORE DECLINES THAN ADVANCES?
WHERE DO I SIGN UP FOR THIS SCHOOL?

BABOYITO, HIJO, I WOULDN'T LIKE IT IF YOU GO TO SCHOOL IN AMERICA AND START HIDING YOUR GRADES FROM ME.
MOMMY, PATO-TEN THE DUCK SAID I CAN DEVISE A NEW REPORT CARD JUST FOR YOU.
IT WILL SHOW ONLY THE ABSOLUTE VALUE OF THE NET OF ADVANCES VERSUS THE DECLINES, DIVIDED BY MY WEIGHT THAT WEEK.
HIJO, WOULDN'T THAT LOOK LIKE YOU'RE COOKING THE BOOKS?
WELL, MOMMY, IT WOULDN'T BE AMERICA IF I DIDN'T COOK THE BOOKS, WOULD IT?
AH, WHAT A TRAINING FOR THE REAL WORLD.

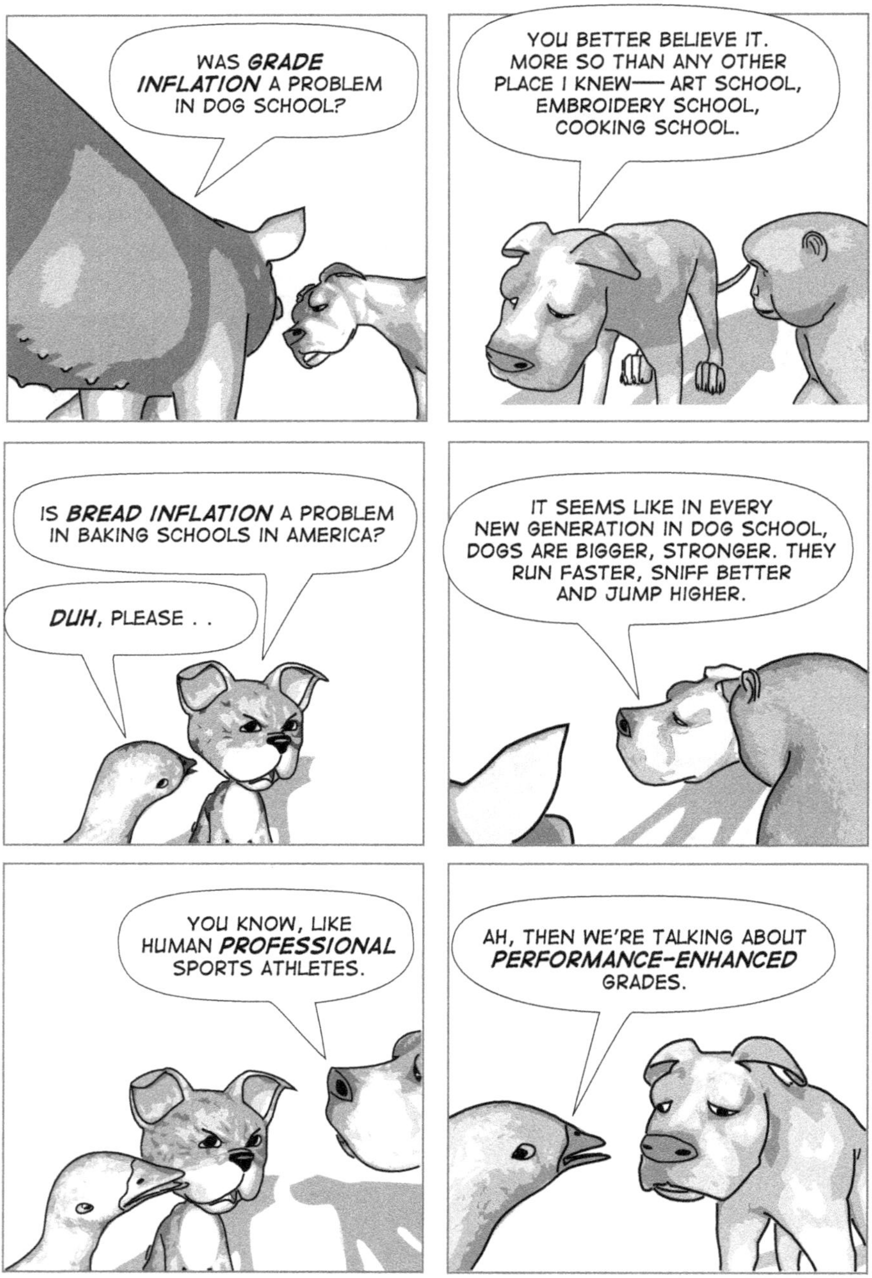
WAS GRADE INFLATION A PROBLEM IN DOG SCHOOL?
YOU BETTER BELIEVE IT. MORE SO THAN ANY OTHER PLACE I KNEW— ART SCHOOL, EMBROIDERY SCHOOL, COOKING SCHOOL.
IS BREAD INFLATION A PROBLEM IN BAKING SCHOOLS IN AMERICA?
DUH, PLEASE . .
IT SEEMS LIKE IN EVERY NEW GENERATION IN DOG SCHOOL, DOGS ARE BIGGER, STRONGER. THEY RUN FASTER, SNIFF BETTER AND JUMP HIGHER.
YOU KNOW, LIKE HUMAN PROFESSIONAL SPORTS ATHLETES.
AH, THEN WE'RE TALKING ABOUT PERFORMANCE-ENHANCED GRADES.

MY MOM IS ALWAYS ASKING WHEN I'M GONNA GET DONE WITH SCHOOL.
SHE MEANS WELL BUT SHE'S LIKE ONE OF THOSE PESKY HUMAN TOTS ON A FAMILY ROAD TRIP WHO'S ALWAYS ASKING "ARE WE THERE YET?"
AMIGO, MAYBE IT'S BECAUSE YOU'RE NOT TELLING HER HOW YOU'RE DOING.
I WANT TO BUT I'M AFRAID SHE'D GET MAD AT ME.
ARE YOU AFRAID SHE MIGHT NOT UNDER-STAND WHAT'S ON YOUR REPORT CARD?
SHE UNDERSTANDS WHAT AN "A" MEANS, A "B," OR AN "F". BUT HOW DO I EXPLAIN AN "F" PLUS ?

Math, Math and More Math

AS AN *ASIAN* IMMIGRANT DOG, DID YOU FEEL PRESSURE TO EXCEL IN *MATH*?
THERE IS THAT PERCEPTION THAT IF A DOG LIKE ME GETS A "*C*" IN MATH, THAT'S LIKE AN "*F*" BY *ASIAN* STANDARDS.
WHAT IF YOU GET A "*D*"? WOULD THAT BE AN "*A*" BY AMERICAN STANDARDS?
A SO-CALLED GENTLEMAN'S "*D*" COULD MEAN MERCY, OR *BRIBERY*.
WHAT IF YOU GET ALL *D*'S? CAN YOU STILL CALL YOURSELF *EDUCATED*?
SURE, YOU'RE EDUCATED, JUST *ALPHABET-IMPAIRED*.

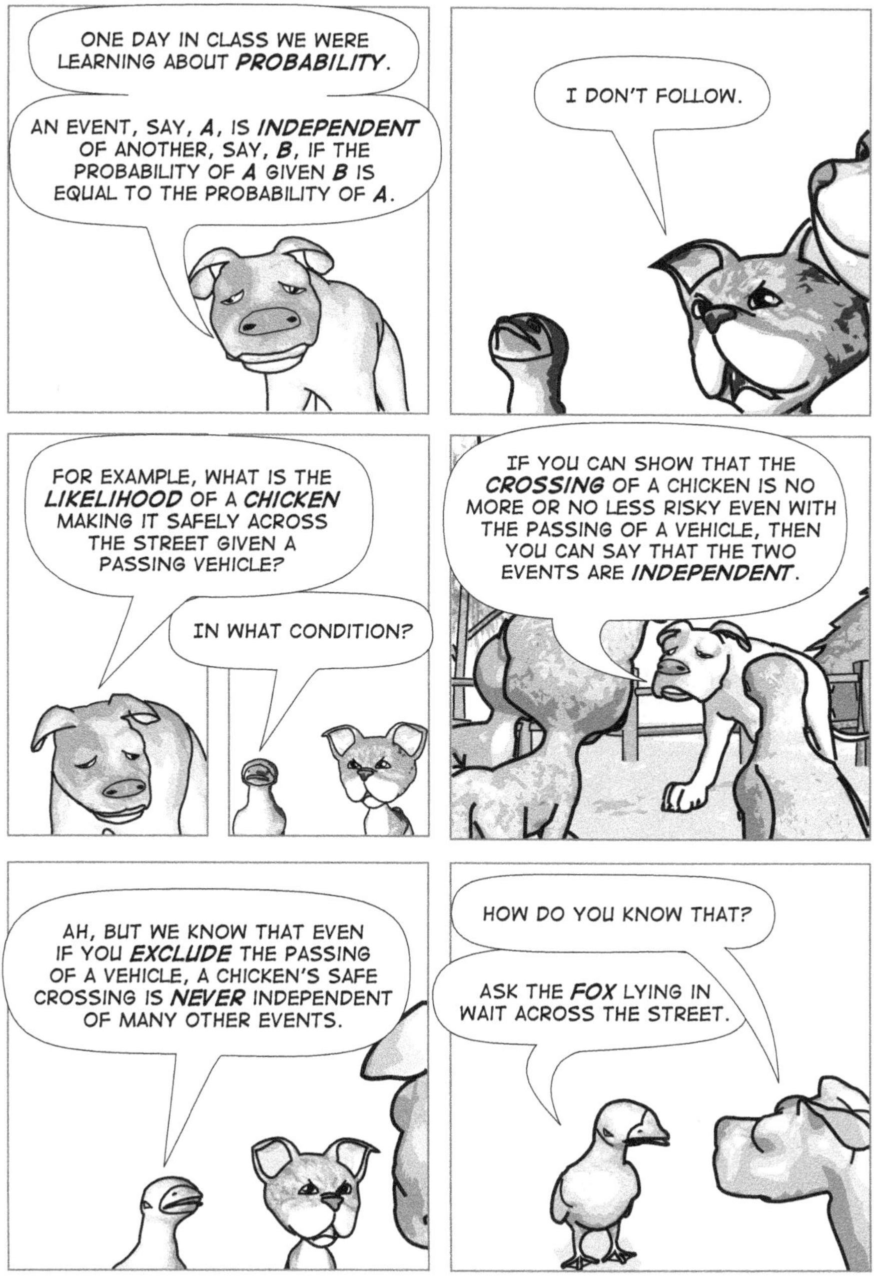
ONE DAY IN CLASS WE WERE LEARNING ABOUT ***PROBABILITY***.
AN EVENT, SAY, ***A***, IS ***INDEPENDENT*** OF ANOTHER, SAY, ***B***, IF THE PROBABILITY OF ***A*** GIVEN ***B*** IS EQUAL TO THE PROBABILITY OF ***A***.
I DON'T FOLLOW.
FOR EXAMPLE, WHAT IS THE ***LIKELIHOOD*** OF A ***CHICKEN*** MAKING IT SAFELY ACROSS THE STREET GIVEN A PASSING VEHICLE?
IN WHAT CONDITION?
IF YOU CAN SHOW THAT THE ***CROSSING*** OF A CHICKEN IS NO MORE OR NO LESS RISKY EVEN WITH THE PASSING OF A VEHICLE, THEN YOU CAN SAY THAT THE TWO EVENTS ARE ***INDEPENDENT***.
AH, BUT WE KNOW THAT EVEN IF YOU ***EXCLUDE*** THE PASSING OF A VEHICLE, A CHICKEN'S SAFE CROSSING IS ***NEVER*** INDEPENDENT OF MANY OTHER EVENTS.
HOW DO YOU KNOW THAT?
ASK THE ***FOX*** LYING IN WAIT ACROSS THE STREET.

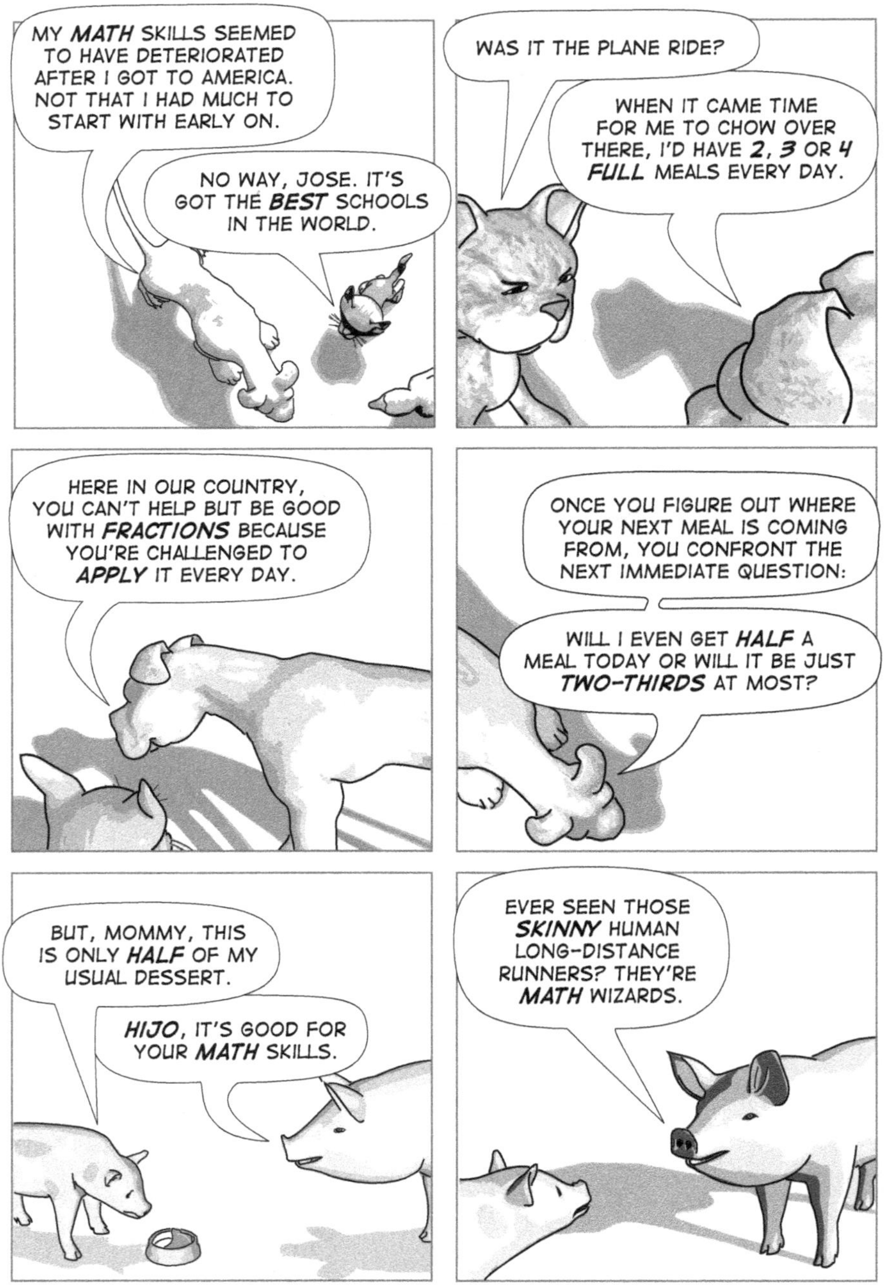
MY MATH SKILLS SEEMED TO HAVE DETERIORATED AFTER I GOT TO AMERICA. NOT THAT I HAD MUCH TO START WITH EARLY ON.
NO WAY, JOSE. IT'S GOT THE BEST SCHOOLS IN THE WORLD.
WAS IT THE PLANE RIDE?
WHEN IT CAME TIME FOR ME TO CHOW OVER THERE, I'D HAVE 2, 3 OR 4 FULL MEALS EVERY DAY.
HERE IN OUR COUNTRY, YOU CAN'T HELP BUT BE GOOD WITH FRACTIONS BECAUSE YOU'RE CHALLENGED TO APPLY IT EVERY DAY.
ONCE YOU FIGURE OUT WHERE YOUR NEXT MEAL IS COMING FROM, YOU CONFRONT THE NEXT IMMEDIATE QUESTION:
WILL I EVEN GET HALF A MEAL TODAY OR WILL IT BE JUST TWO-THIRDS AT MOST?
BUT, MOMMY, THIS IS ONLY HALF OF MY USUAL DESSERT.
HIJO, IT'S GOOD FOR YOUR MATH SKILLS.
EVER SEEN THOSE SKINNY HUMAN LONG-DISTANCE RUNNERS? THEY'RE MATH WIZARDS.

Technology

TECHNOLOGY CAN BE YOUR ENEMY. I WASN'T HAPPY WHEN MY MASTER BOUGHT AN ALARM SYSTEM FOR THE HOUSE. I WANTED HER TO GET A LOW-TECH SOLUTION— ME.
AN ALARM SYSTEM CAN'T TELL A HUMAN PARENT IF HER TEENAGER SKIPPED SCHOOL AND SNEAKED HOME.
AND YOU EXPECTED TO DO THAT, TELL ON THE KID?
NO. IN AMERICA, THAT'S THE JOB OF THE NOSY NEIGHBORS.

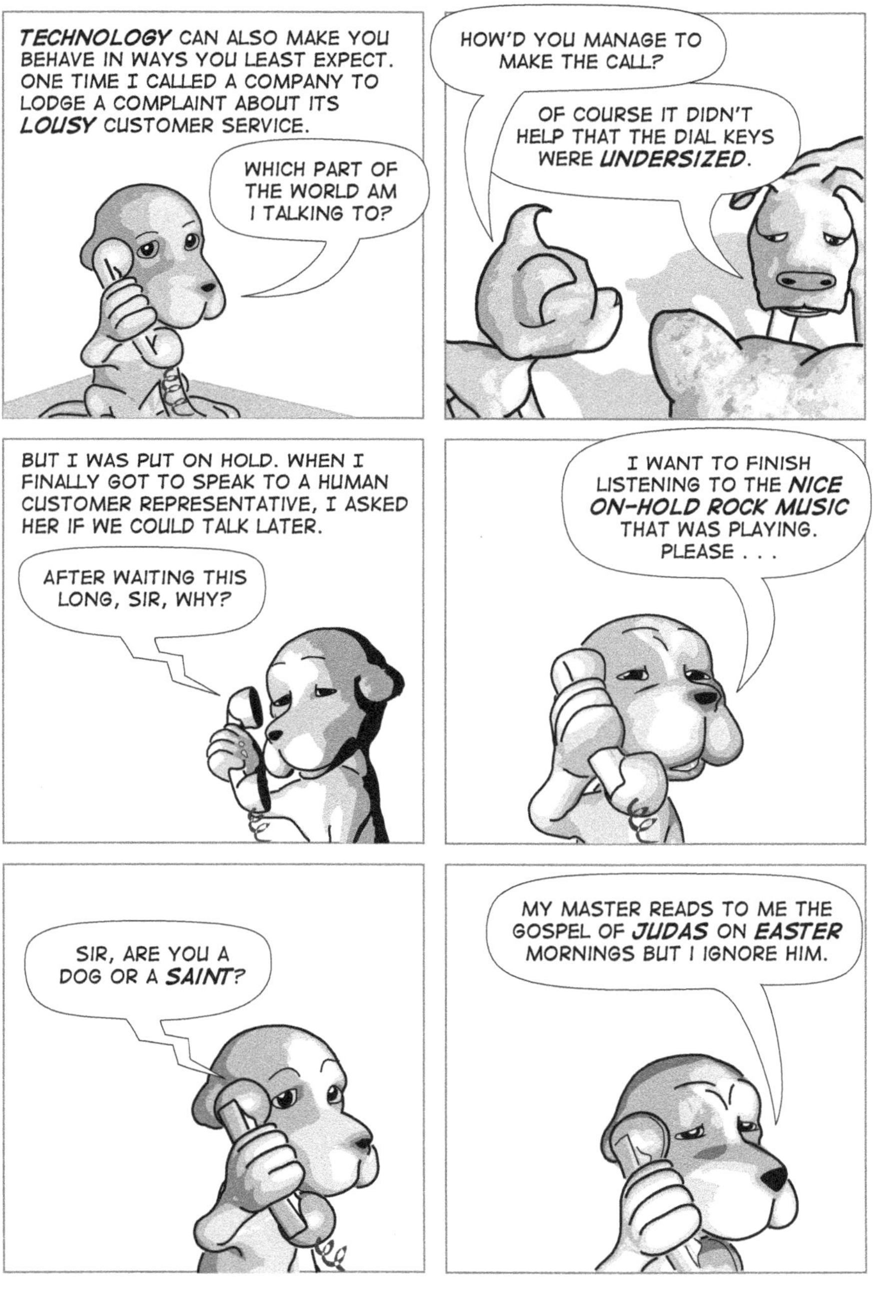
TECHNOLOGY CAN ALSO MAKE YOU BEHAVE IN WAYS YOU LEAST EXPECT. ONE TIME I CALLED A COMPANY TO LODGE A COMPLAINT ABOUT ITS LOUSY CUSTOMER SERVICE.
WHICH PART OF THE WORLD AM I TALKING TO?
HOW'D YOU MANAGE TO MAKE THE CALL?
OF COURSE IT DIDN'T HELP THAT THE DIAL KEYS WERE UNDERSIZED.
BUT I WAS PUT ON HOLD. WHEN I FINALLY GOT TO SPEAK TO A HUMAN CUSTOMER REPRESENTATIVE, I ASKED HER IF WE COULD TALK LATER.
AFTER WAITING THIS LONG, SIR, WHY?
I WANT TO FINISH LISTENING TO THE NICE ON-HOLD ROCK MUSIC THAT WAS PLAYING. PLEASE . . .
SIR, ARE YOU A DOG OR A SAINT?
MY MASTER READS TO ME THE GOSPEL OF JUDAS ON EASTER MORNINGS BUT I IGNORE HIM.

Ccreativity in the Classroom

WERE YOU ALLOWED TO BE *CREATIVE* IN OBEDIENCE SCHOOL?

DID YOUR TRAINERS OR HANDLERS LET YOU DRAW *OUTSIDE* THE LINES?

THEY LET US DRAW *OUTSIDE* THE LINES, . . .

. . . *OFF* THE PAPER, *ON* THE DESKTOP, . . .

. . . *UNDER* THE DESK, *ON* ITS LEGS, . . .

. . . *AROUND IT, ON* LUNCHBOXES, . . .

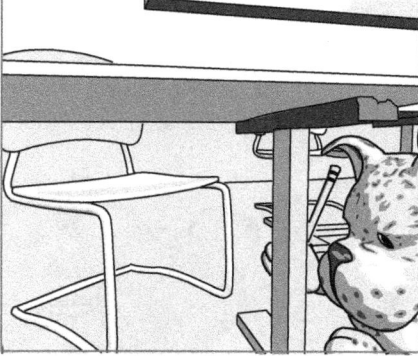

. . . *DOWN ON* THE FLOOR, . . .

. . . *ON* THE WALLS, . . .

. . . *ALONG* THE CORRIDOR, *ALL* THE WAY TO THE PLAYGROUND *ALL* THE TIME UNTIL *RECESS*.

OUR TRAINERS AND I DIDN'T ALWAYS SEE EYE TO EYE.

THEY WANTED US TO GO OUTSIDE OFTEN, OUT IN THE PLAYGROUND OR ON THE FIELD, TO **BROADEN** OUR THINKING, EXPAND OUR HORIZON.

LIKE THE ANCIENT *GREEK* PHILOSOPHERS, THEY WANTED TO TEACH US BY *WALKING AROUND* WITH THEIR STUDENTS, CONVERSING, OFTEN GESTURING TOWARD THE SKY TO MAKE A POINT.

I WANTED TO STAY IN THE CLASSROOM ESPECIALLY WHEN IT WAS COLD OUT. I WANTED TO BE SURROUNDED BY WALLS DECORATED WITH MY **STARRED** WORK AND THOSE OF MY CLASSMATES.

I WANTED TO THINK *INSIDE* THE BOX.

72

Globalization

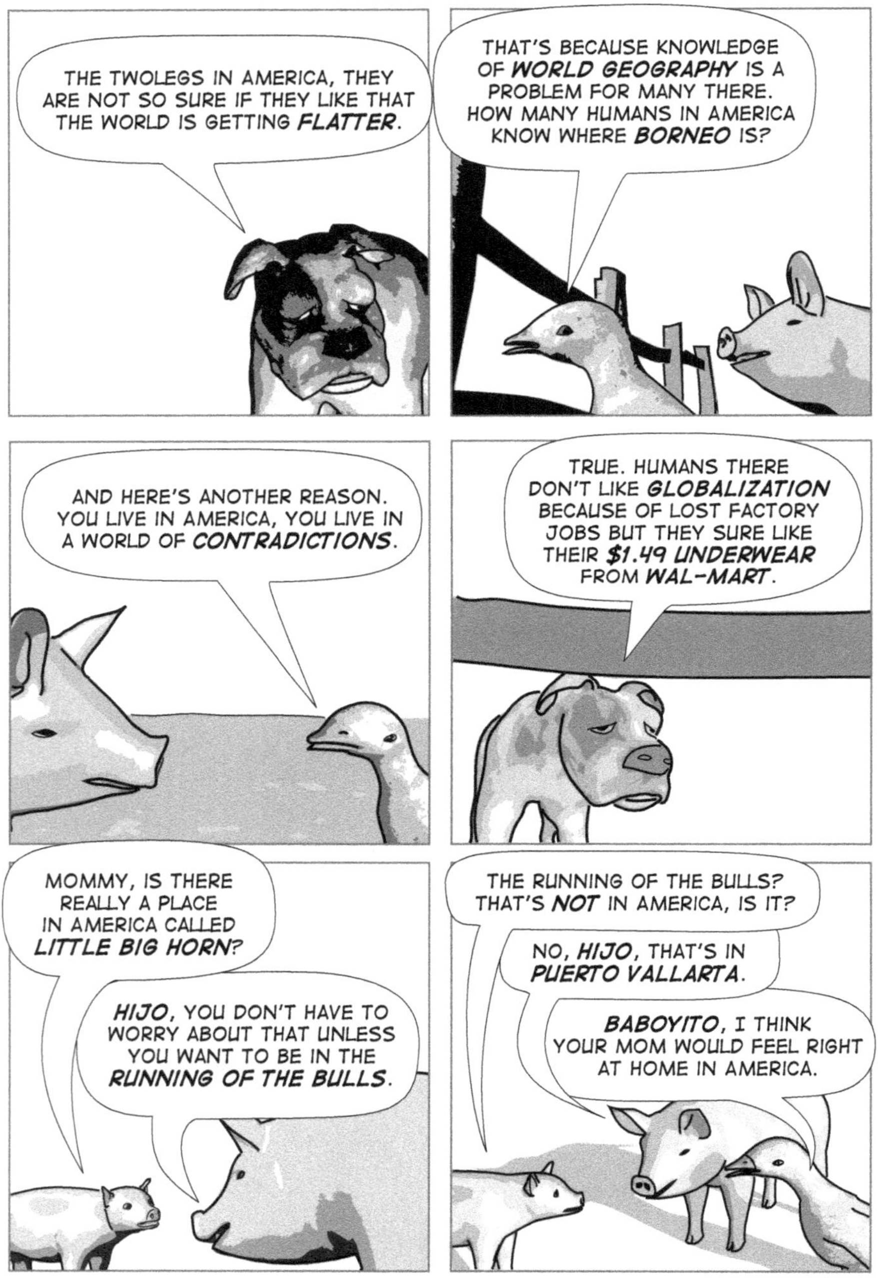
THE TWOLEGS IN AMERICA, THEY ARE NOT SO SURE IF THEY LIKE THAT THE WORLD IS GETTING *FLATTER*.
THAT'S BECAUSE KNOWLEDGE OF *WORLD GEOGRAPHY* IS A PROBLEM FOR MANY THERE. HOW MANY HUMANS IN AMERICA KNOW WHERE *BORNEO* IS?
AND HERE'S ANOTHER REASON. YOU LIVE IN AMERICA, YOU LIVE IN A WORLD OF *CONTRADICTIONS*.
TRUE. HUMANS THERE DON'T LIKE *GLOBALIZATION* BECAUSE OF LOST FACTORY JOBS BUT THEY SURE LIKE THEIR *$1.49 UNDERWEAR* FROM *WAL-MART*.
MOMMY, IS THERE REALLY A PLACE IN AMERICA CALLED *LITTLE BIG HORN*?
HIJO, YOU DON'T HAVE TO WORRY ABOUT THAT UNLESS YOU WANT TO BE IN THE *RUNNING OF THE BULLS*.
THE RUNNING OF THE BULLS? THAT'S *NOT* IN AMERICA, IS IT?
NO, *HIJO*, THAT'S IN *PUERTO VALLARTA*.
BABOYITO, I THINK YOUR MOM WOULD FEEL RIGHT AT HOME IN AMERICA.

WE WERE TAUGHT IN OUR ECONOMICS CLASS THAT TRADE IS IMPORTANT.
IT LETS YOU RAISE YOUR STANDARD OF LIVING, MAKES YOU BETTER OFF.
DID YOU EXCHANGE LUNCH WITH YOUR DOG CLASSMATES IN SCHOOL?
I WANTED TO BUT MY AMERICAN DOG CLASSMATES WOULDN'T TRADE LUNCH WITH ME. I WAS PUZZLED AND HURT.
I KNOW WHY. DON'T TELL ME. THEY MUST HAVE BEEN SICK OF YOUR LUNCH OF SEVERAL-DAY LEFTOVER RAMEN NOODLES WHICH THEY COULD SNIFF OUT A MILE AWAY.
CORRECTION: THEY'RE REGURGITATED SEVERAL-DAY LEFTOVER RAMEN NOODLES.

Edifice Complex

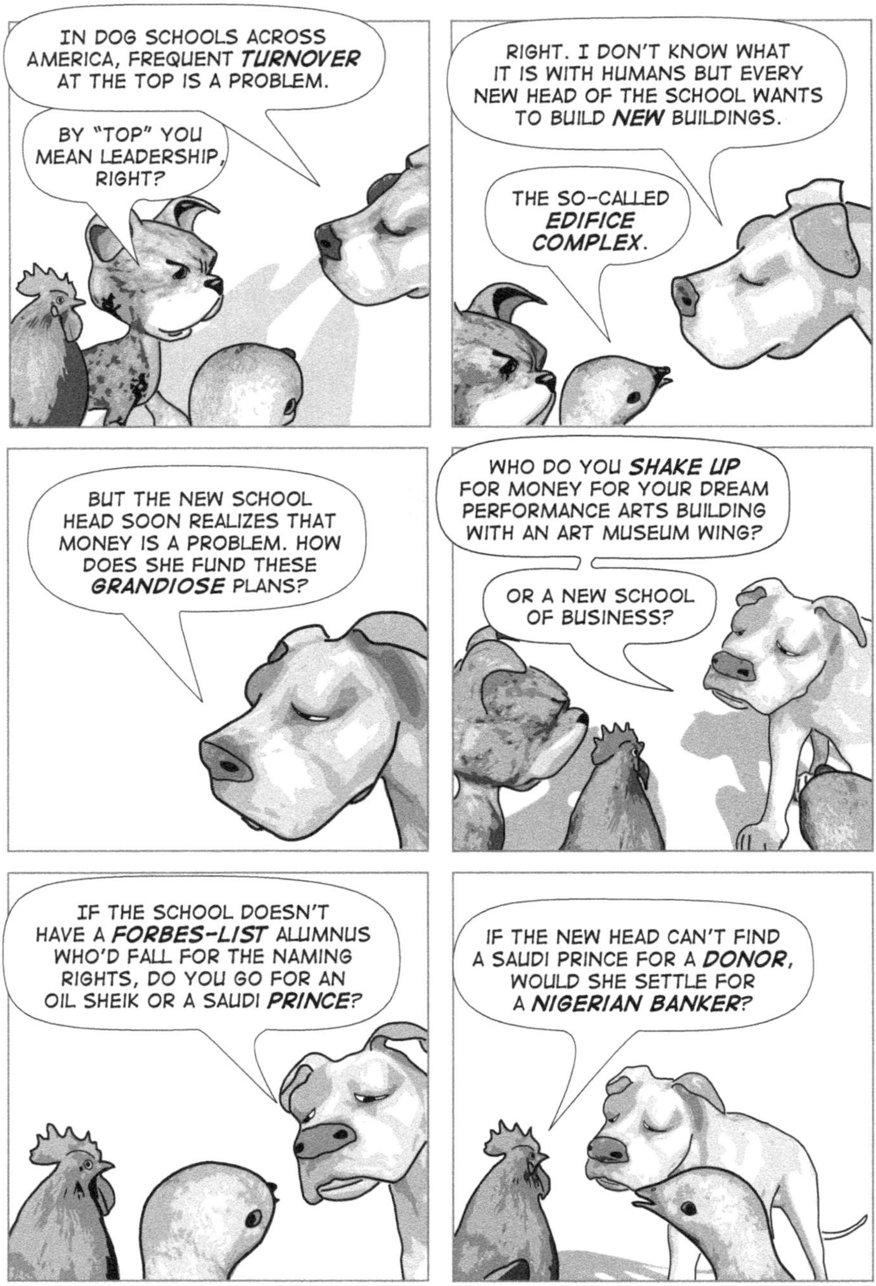
IN DOG SCHOOLS ACROSS AMERICA, FREQUENT ***TURNOVER*** AT THE TOP IS A PROBLEM.
BY "TOP" YOU MEAN LEADERSHIP, RIGHT?
RIGHT. I DON'T KNOW WHAT IT IS WITH HUMANS BUT EVERY NEW HEAD OF THE SCHOOL WANTS TO BUILD ***NEW*** BUILDINGS.
THE SO-CALLED ***EDIFICE COMPLEX***.
BUT THE NEW SCHOOL HEAD SOON REALIZES THAT MONEY IS A PROBLEM. HOW DOES SHE FUND THESE ***GRANDIOSE*** PLANS?
WHO DO YOU ***SHAKE UP*** FOR MONEY FOR YOUR DREAM PERFORMANCE ARTS BUILDING WITH AN ART MUSEUM WING?
OR A NEW SCHOOL OF BUSINESS?
IF THE SCHOOL DOESN'T HAVE A ***FORBES-LIST*** ALUMNUS WHO'D FALL FOR THE NAMING RIGHTS, DO YOU GO FOR AN OIL SHEIK OR A SAUDI ***PRINCE***?
IF THE NEW HEAD CAN'T FIND A SAUDI PRINCE FOR A ***DONOR***, WOULD SHE SETTLE FOR A ***NIGERIAN BANKER***?

MOMMY, DID THE THREE LITTLE PIGS HAVE AN EDIFICE COMPLEX?
I'M SORRY, HIJO, I DON'T FOLLOW.
YOU KNOW. ONE PIG BUILT A HOUSE OF TWIGS, ANOTHER BUILT A HOUSE OF STRAWS, AND THE THIRD A HOUSE OF BRICKS.
AND WHAT DID YOU CALL IT AGAIN?
EDIFICE COMPLEX.
YOUR SLIGHT MISPRONUNCIATION ASIDE, AN OEDIPUS COMPLEX IS MORE COMPLEX THAN JUST HOME BUILDING.

East versus West

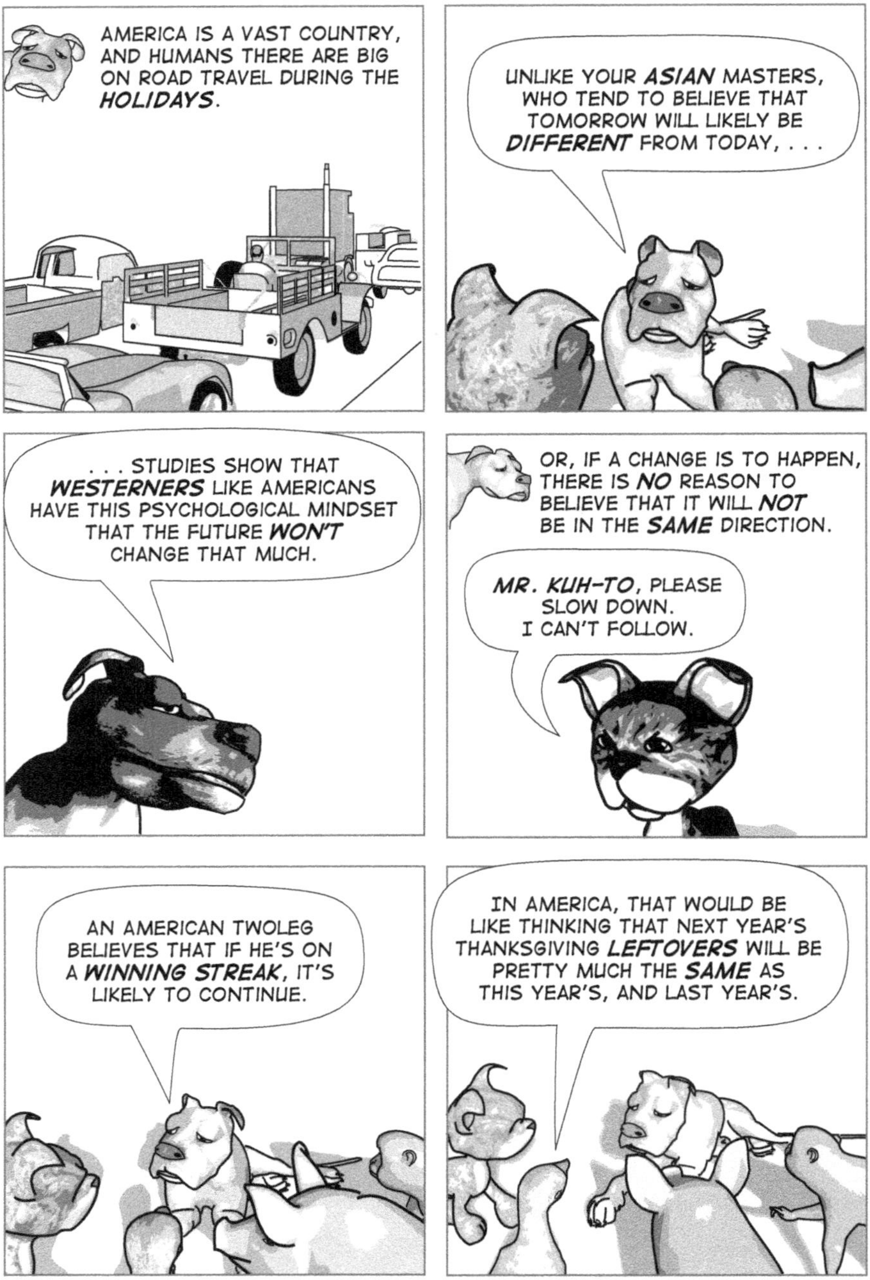
AMERICA IS A VAST COUNTRY, AND HUMANS THERE ARE BIG ON ROAD TRAVEL DURING THE HOLIDAYS.
UNLIKE YOUR ASIAN MASTERS, WHO TEND TO BELIEVE THAT TOMORROW WILL LIKELY BE DIFFERENT FROM TODAY, . . .
. . . STUDIES SHOW THAT WESTERNERS LIKE AMERICANS HAVE THIS PSYCHOLOGICAL MINDSET THAT THE FUTURE WON'T CHANGE THAT MUCH.
OR, IF A CHANGE IS TO HAPPEN, THERE IS NO REASON TO BELIEVE THAT IT WILL NOT BE IN THE SAME DIRECTION.
MR. KUH-TO, PLEASE SLOW DOWN. I CAN'T FOLLOW.
AN AMERICAN TWOLEG BELIEVES THAT IF HE'S ON A WINNING STREAK, IT'S LIKELY TO CONTINUE.
IN AMERICA, THAT WOULD BE LIKE THINKING THAT NEXT YEAR'S THANKSGIVING LEFTOVERS WILL BE PRETTY MUCH THE SAME AS THIS YEAR'S, AND LAST YEAR'S.

PRETTY GRIM, HUH?

I THOUGHT YOU LIKE *STABILITY* IN YOUR FOOD SUPPLY.

EASTERNERS ON THE OTHER HAND ARE INCLINED TO THINK THAT IF EVERYONE'S DOING WELL, IT'S TIME TO *SELL* YOUR HOUSE BECAUSE A *REVERSAL* OF FORTUNE LOOMS AHEAD.

EVEN IF IT'S 'UNDERWATER'?

SO YOU'RE SAYING SO AS NOT TO DISRUPT THEIR HOLIDAY DRIVING AND SAVE THEM THE TROUBLE, . . .

. . . IT MAY BE A GOOD IDEA FOR AMERICAN TWOLEGS TO GET *AND* PAY THEIR SPEEDING TICKETS *AHEAD* OF TIME?

HOW FAR AHEAD? IS *FIVE* YEARS ENOUGH?

Adjusting to the American Way

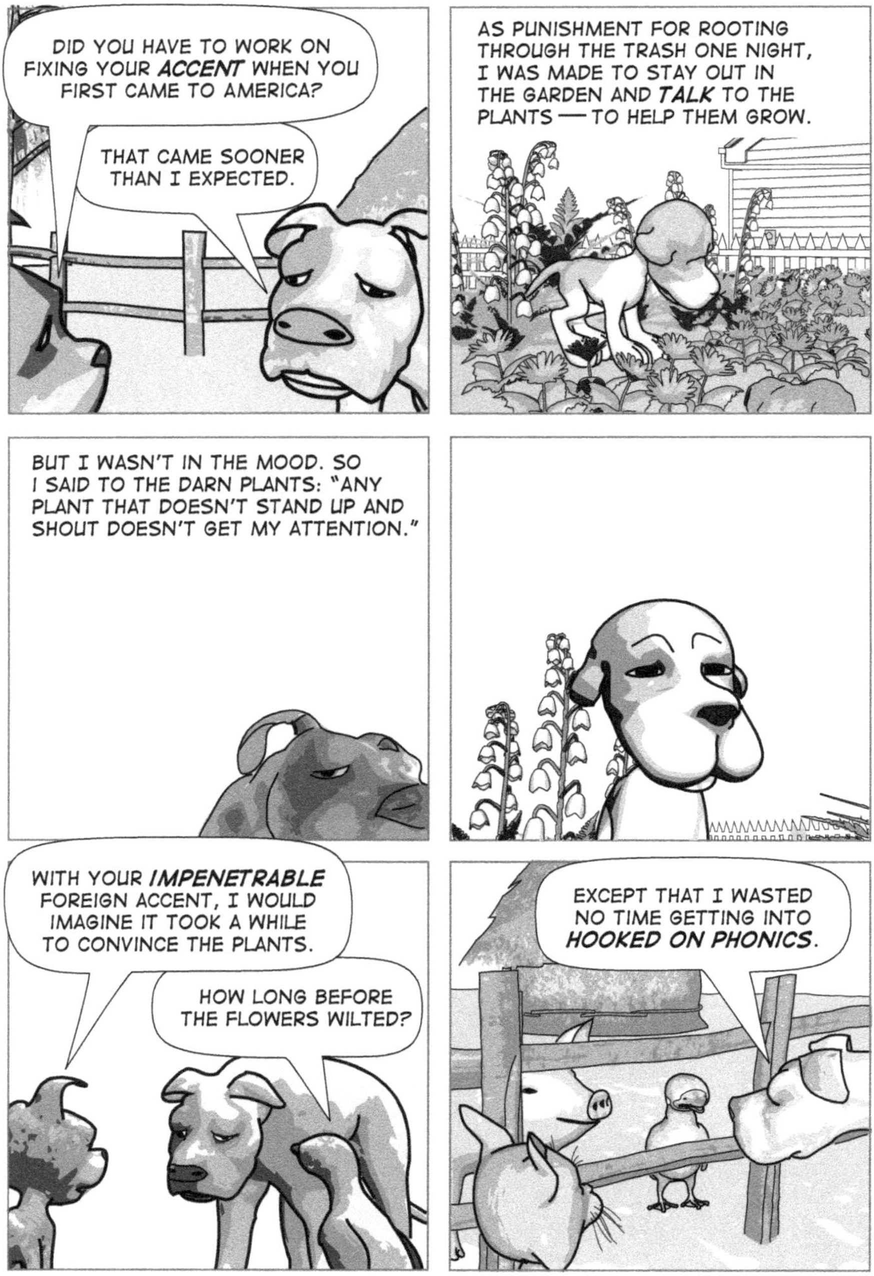
DID YOU HAVE TO WORK ON FIXING YOUR *ACCENT* WHEN YOU FIRST CAME TO AMERICA?
THAT CAME SOONER THAN I EXPECTED.
AS PUNISHMENT FOR ROOTING THROUGH THE TRASH ONE NIGHT, I WAS MADE TO STAY OUT IN THE GARDEN AND *TALK* TO THE PLANTS — TO HELP THEM GROW.
BUT I WASN'T IN THE MOOD. SO I SAID TO THE DARN PLANTS: "ANY PLANT THAT DOESN'T STAND UP AND SHOUT DOESN'T GET MY ATTENTION."
WITH YOUR *IMPENETRABLE* FOREIGN ACCENT, I WOULD IMAGINE IT TOOK A WHILE TO CONVINCE THE PLANTS.
HOW LONG BEFORE THE FLOWERS WILTED?
EXCEPT THAT I WASTED NO TIME GETTING INTO ***HOOKED ON PHONICS***.

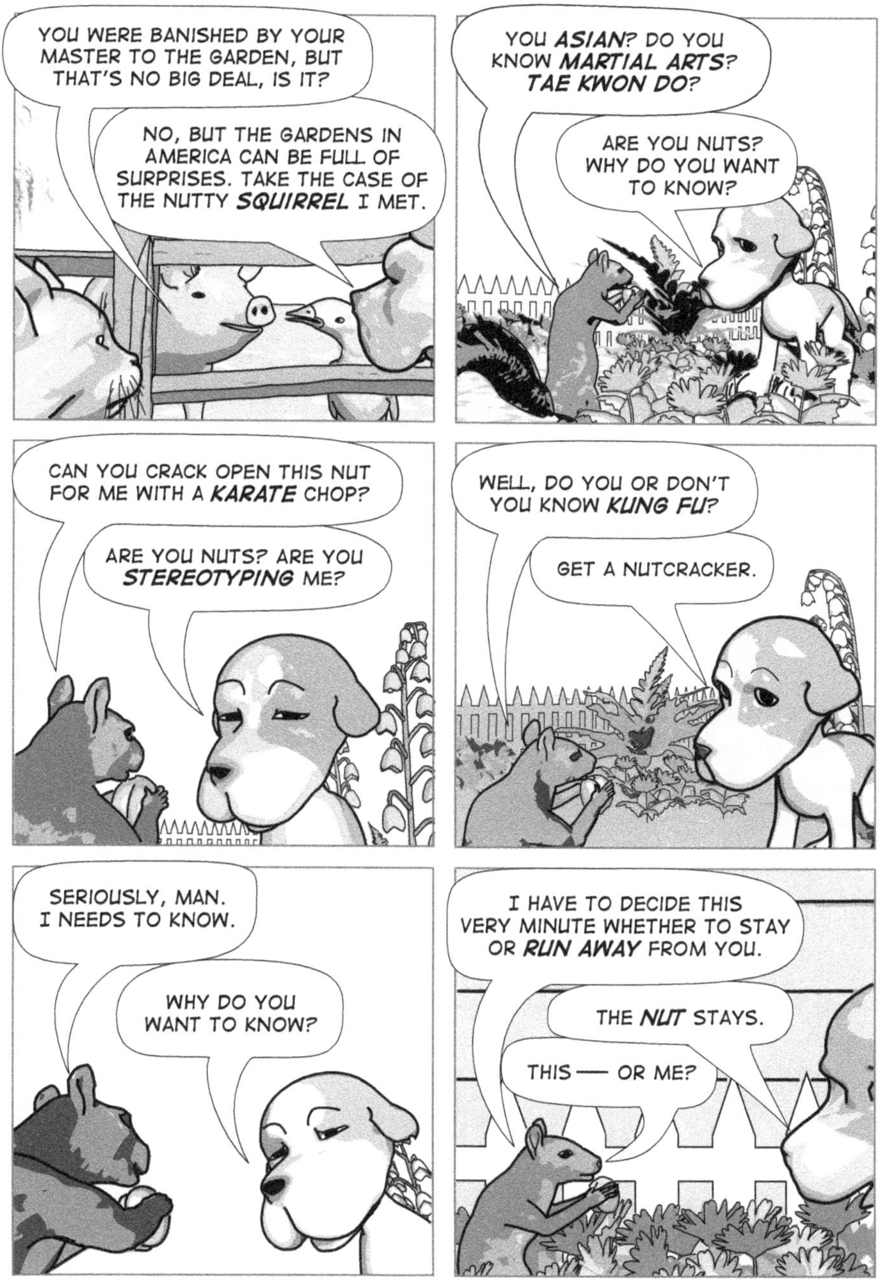
YOU WERE BANISHED BY YOUR MASTER TO THE GARDEN, BUT THAT'S NO BIG DEAL, IS IT?
NO, BUT THE GARDENS IN AMERICA CAN BE FULL OF SURPRISES. TAKE THE CASE OF THE NUTTY SQUIRREL I MET.
YOU ASIAN? DO YOU KNOW MARTIAL ARTS? TAE KWON DO?
ARE YOU NUTS? WHY DO YOU WANT TO KNOW?
CAN YOU CRACK OPEN THIS NUT FOR ME WITH A KARATE CHOP?
ARE YOU NUTS? ARE YOU STEREOTYPING ME?
WELL, DO YOU OR DON'T YOU KNOW KUNG FU?
GET A NUTCRACKER.
SERIOUSLY, MAN. I NEEDS TO KNOW.
WHY DO YOU WANT TO KNOW?
I HAVE TO DECIDE THIS VERY MINUTE WHETHER TO STAY OR RUN AWAY FROM YOU.
THE NUT STAYS.
THIS — OR ME?

Rat Race

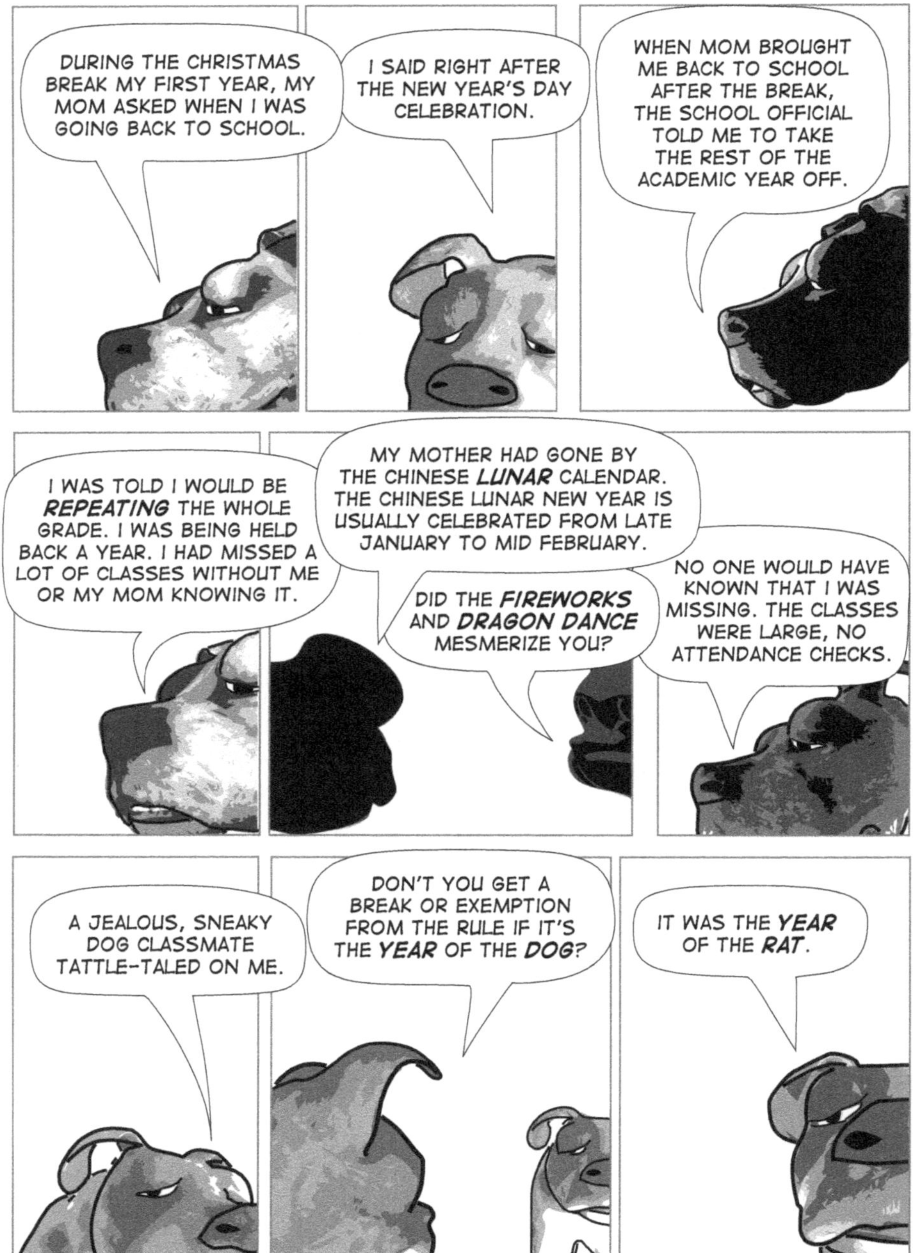
DURING THE CHRISTMAS BREAK MY FIRST YEAR, MY MOM ASKED WHEN I WAS GOING BACK TO SCHOOL.
I SAID RIGHT AFTER THE NEW YEAR'S DAY CELEBRATION.
WHEN MOM BROUGHT ME BACK TO SCHOOL AFTER THE BREAK, THE SCHOOL OFFICIAL TOLD ME TO TAKE THE REST OF THE ACADEMIC YEAR OFF.
I WAS TOLD I WOULD BE *REPEATING* THE WHOLE GRADE. I WAS BEING HELD BACK A YEAR. I HAD MISSED A LOT OF CLASSES WITHOUT ME OR MY MOM KNOWING IT.
MY MOTHER HAD GONE BY THE CHINESE *LUNAR* CALENDAR. THE CHINESE LUNAR NEW YEAR IS USUALLY CELEBRATED FROM LATE JANUARY TO MID FEBRUARY.
DID THE *FIREWORKS* AND *DRAGON DANCE* MESMERIZE YOU?
NO ONE WOULD HAVE KNOWN THAT I WAS MISSING. THE CLASSES WERE LARGE, NO ATTENDANCE CHECKS.
A JEALOUS, SNEAKY DOG CLASSMATE TATTLE-TALED ON ME.
DON'T YOU GET A BREAK OR EXEMPTION FROM THE RULE IF IT'S THE *YEAR* OF THE *DOG*?
IT WAS THE *YEAR* OF THE *RAT*.

I ONCE MET A *RAT* WHO WORKED IN A TESTING LAB IN AMERICA.
BORING, REPETITIVE TASKS, MEAGER RATIONS; A DANGEROUS JOB, DUDE. YOU CAN'T EVEN ASK IF WHAT YOU'RE DOING IS REALLY IN YOUR ***JOB DESCRIPTION***.
BUT HE WAS MOSTLY WORRIED ABOUT GLOBALIZATION, OUTSOURCING.
THERE ARE MILLIONS OF RATS IN CHINA WILLING TO COME TO WORK IN AMERICA FOR EVEN LESS.
I MEAN, FOR ABSOLUTELY NOTHING. NADA. ZIP.
WHAT COULD BE LESS THAN NOTHING— DYING ON THE STREET KNOWING YOU'RE ***BEHIND*** ON YOUR RENT?
HM, YOU MAY NOT BE THAT FAR FROM THE TRUTH. DO YOU THINK I SHOULD CUT MY LOSSES NOW?
DEPENDS. HOW SOON WOULD A MILLION RATS FROM CHINA BE CROSSING THE BORDER?
HM . . . WHAT PERCENT IS THAT OF ***1.34 BILLION***?

BUT RATS ARE USED TO WORKING FOR LESS. WHAT DID HE EXPECT — A BETTER OFFER?
YEAH. IT'S AMERICA, DUDE. WHY DO YOU THINK THEY CALL IT A ***RAT RACE*** OVER THERE?
LIKE YOU, I'M AN IMMIGRANT, TOO. BUT UNLIKE YOU, I HAVE MOUTHS TO FEED.
I FELT A SENSE OF COMPASSION FOR THE POOR ANIMAL. I OFFERED TO TREAT HIM TO THE GARBAGE AT HOME.
NO, THANKS. IT'S ***HUMILIATING***.
WHAT DID HE EXPECT, A ***TEA CEREMONY***?
I DON'T BELIEVE IT. HE REFUSED THE ***REFUSE***.
WHY DO YOU THINK THE RAT WAS PICKY?
NATURAL SELECTION?
MAYBE BECAUSE HE WASN'T OFFERED A ***HIGHCHAIR***?
I THINK THE RAT ONLY LIKES FOOD IN SHADES OF ***YELLOW***, WITH ***HOLES*** IN IT — AND A ***TRAP*** NEXT TO IT.

WHAT HAVE YOU READ EVER SINCE YOU CAME TO AMERICA?
I HAVEN'T CRACKED OPEN ANY BOOKS YET BUT I'LL SOON BE STARTING WITH OBEDIENCE SCHOOL.
IN MY NEIGHBORHOOD, EVERY HOUSEHOLD ANIMAL WORTH ITS SALT READS AS A MATTER OF ***SURVIVAL***.
THE DOG . . .
CATS for DUMMIES
THE CAT . . .
DOGS for DUMMIES
MYSELF . . .
ESCAPE from DUMMIES
The Long Tail
. . ., EVERY DAY . . .
THE LONG TAIL
. . ., EVERY NIGHT, . . .
THE AFFAIR OF THE POISONS

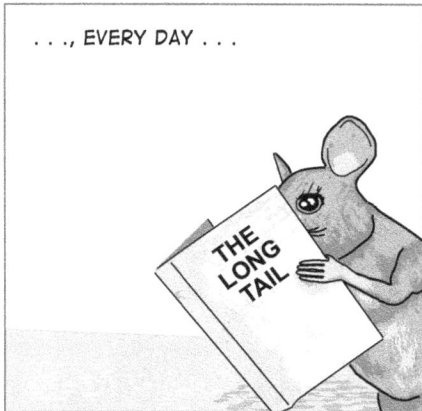

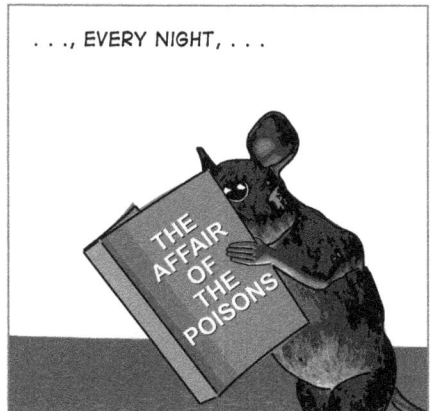

Ant Tribe: Life in the Colony

IF YOU THINK *SPECIALIZATION* IS IMPORTANT IN KEEPING YOUR JOB IN AMERICA, *SUB-SPECIALIZATION* IS EVEN MORE CRITICAL. TAKE THE ANTS.

LOOK, THE ANTS HAVE FORMED A *BEELINE*. MAYBE THEY HAVE FOUND WHERE THE MASTER HID THE *SUGAR*.

THESE ARE NOT JUST *GATHERER* ANTS. LISTEN TO THE HUM OF THEIR FEET. THEY ARE *SHOPPER* ANTS.

HOW DO YOU KNOW?

LOOK, THEY ARE TROOPING TO A BLUE LIGHT *DISCOUNT* SPECIAL BY THE *TRASH*.

AMONG ANTS IN AMERICA, THERE IS A STRICT *SEPARATION* OF FUNCTIONS LEADING TO SUBSPECIALIZATION.
HEY, YOU'RE SUPPOSED TO BE LIFTING *20* TIMES YOUR BODY WEIGHT.
BUT I'M A *QUEEN* ANT.
OKAY, A SHOPPING BAG, OR TWO, IS FINE.
THE *NANO* COMPUTER, IS THAT DUAL-CORE?
YEP. THE SHOPPING BAGS, ARE THEY FROM *IKEA*?
YEP.
NO ASSEMBLY REQUIRED? BATTERIES?

BUT IF YOU'RE A QUEEN ANT, WHY ARE YOU DOING YOUR OWN SHOPPING? DON'T YOU HAVE A PERSONAL SHOPPER?
DON'T YOU THINK YOU SHOULD BE HOME IN THE COLONY BREEDING MORE ANTS?
YOU MEAN MORE SHOPPER ANTS?
WHEN YOU SHOP, ARE YOU A HUNTER OR GATHERER?
BOTH. DEPENDS ON WHAT'S BEING HUNTED OR GATHERED.
AND WHEN YOU BREED MORE SHOPPER ANTS?
THAT'S WHEN I BUY SHARES OF STOCK IN A CREDIT CARD COMPANY.

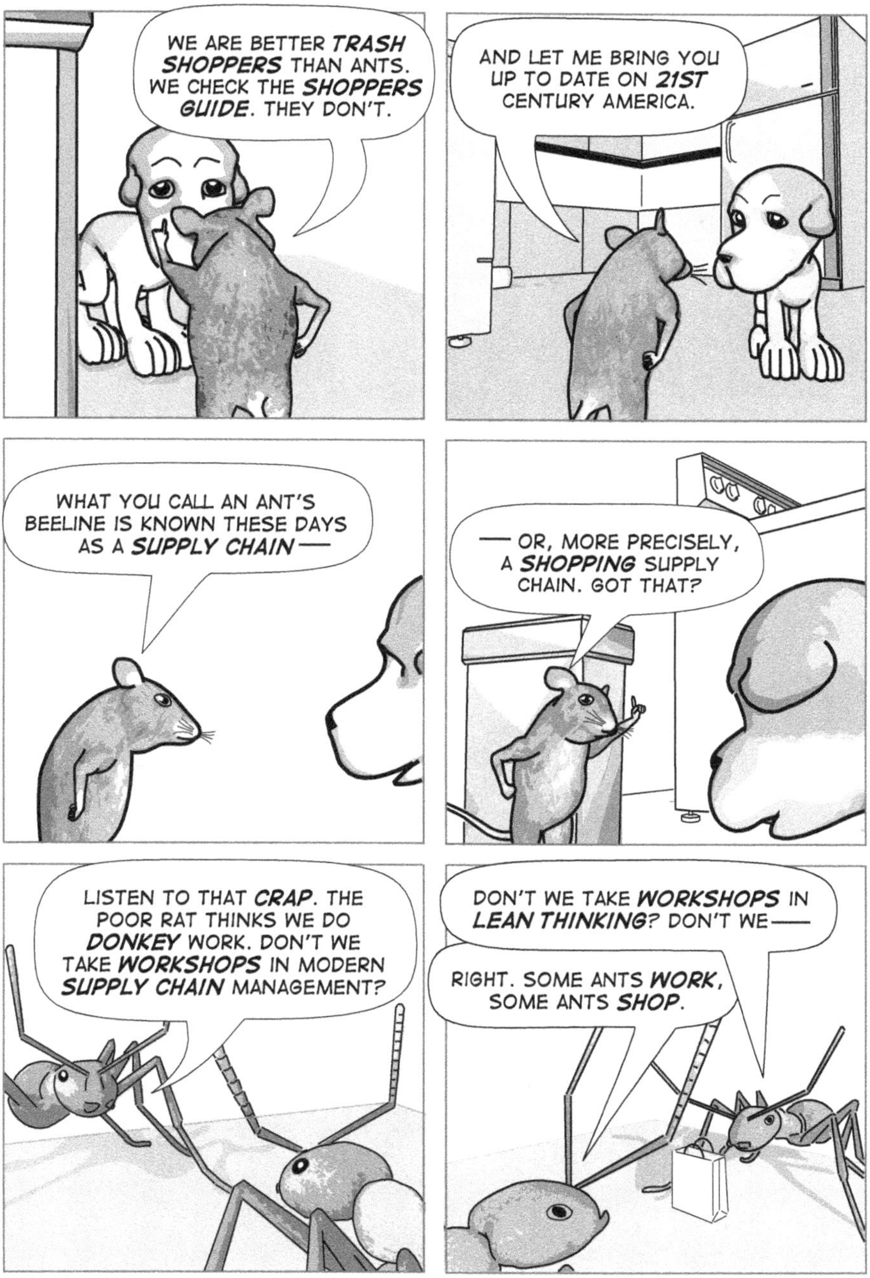
WE ARE BETTER TRASH SHOPPERS THAN ANTS. WE CHECK THE SHOPPERS GUIDE. THEY DON'T.
AND LET ME BRING YOU UP TO DATE ON 21ST CENTURY AMERICA.
WHAT YOU CALL AN ANT'S BEELINE IS KNOWN THESE DAYS AS A SUPPLY CHAIN—
—OR, MORE PRECISELY, A SHOPPING SUPPLY CHAIN. GOT THAT?
LISTEN TO THAT CRAP. THE POOR RAT THINKS WE DO DONKEY WORK. DON'T WE TAKE WORKSHOPS IN MODERN SUPPLY CHAIN MANAGEMENT?
DON'T WE TAKE WORKSHOPS IN LEAN THINKING? DON'T WE—
RIGHT. SOME ANTS WORK, SOME ANTS SHOP.

IT'S HARD BEING AN ALIEN ON A GUEST WORKER PROGRAM HERE IN AMERICA.
I'M ALWAYS TEMPTED TO STAY PERMANENTLY, LEGALLY OR ILLEGALLY. TO LOOK FOR HIGHER-PAYING JOBS.
SO MUCH UNCERTAINTY. YOU CAN'T DECIDE WHICH COLONY TO SETTLE IN. HOW CAN I BUY A 52-INCH FLAT SCREEN TV?
THAT THING'S A MONSTER TO LUG AROUND— MORE THAN 20 TIMES MY BODY WEIGHT.

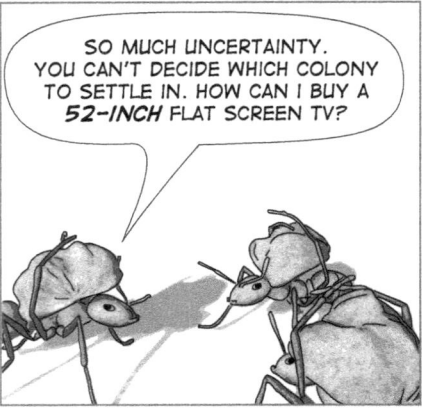

On Gifts

DID YOUR MASTER EVER THINK OF SENDING YOU TO A DOG SCHOOL FOR THE *GIFTED* ?
EVEN AS A PUP I STRUGGLED WITH BEING *HOUSEBROKEN*.
I COULDN'T GET THE HANG OF THE BASICS LIKE 'ROLL OVER,' 'SIT' OR 'STAY.' I REBELLED. I RAN AWAY FROM HOME WHEN I WAS LITTLE.
BECAUSE OF THAT, I WAS STRIPPED OF WHAT LITTLE *INHERITANCE* I HAD. SO, NO.
YOU WEREN'T *GIFTED*?
NO.

IN THE SPIRIT OF THE HOLIDAY SEASON, ***REGIFTING*** AMONG HUMANS IS ALSO BECOMING MORE COMMON IN AMERICA NOWADAYS.
WHAT'S THAT?
REGIFTING IS WHEN YOU GIVE AWAY AS ***YOUR*** PRESENT WHAT SOMEONE ELSE HAD GIVEN YOU AS A GIFT.
THAT'S ***RECYCLING***. YOU'RE RECYCLING TO SOMEONE YOUR UNHAPPINESS WITH THE GIFT— AND YOU CALL THAT GIVING?
NO, IN AMERICA, YOU CALL THAT ***SPRING CLEANING***.
ARE YOU SAYING ALL GARBAGE COLLECTORS ARE ***GIFTED***?

Household Hierarchy

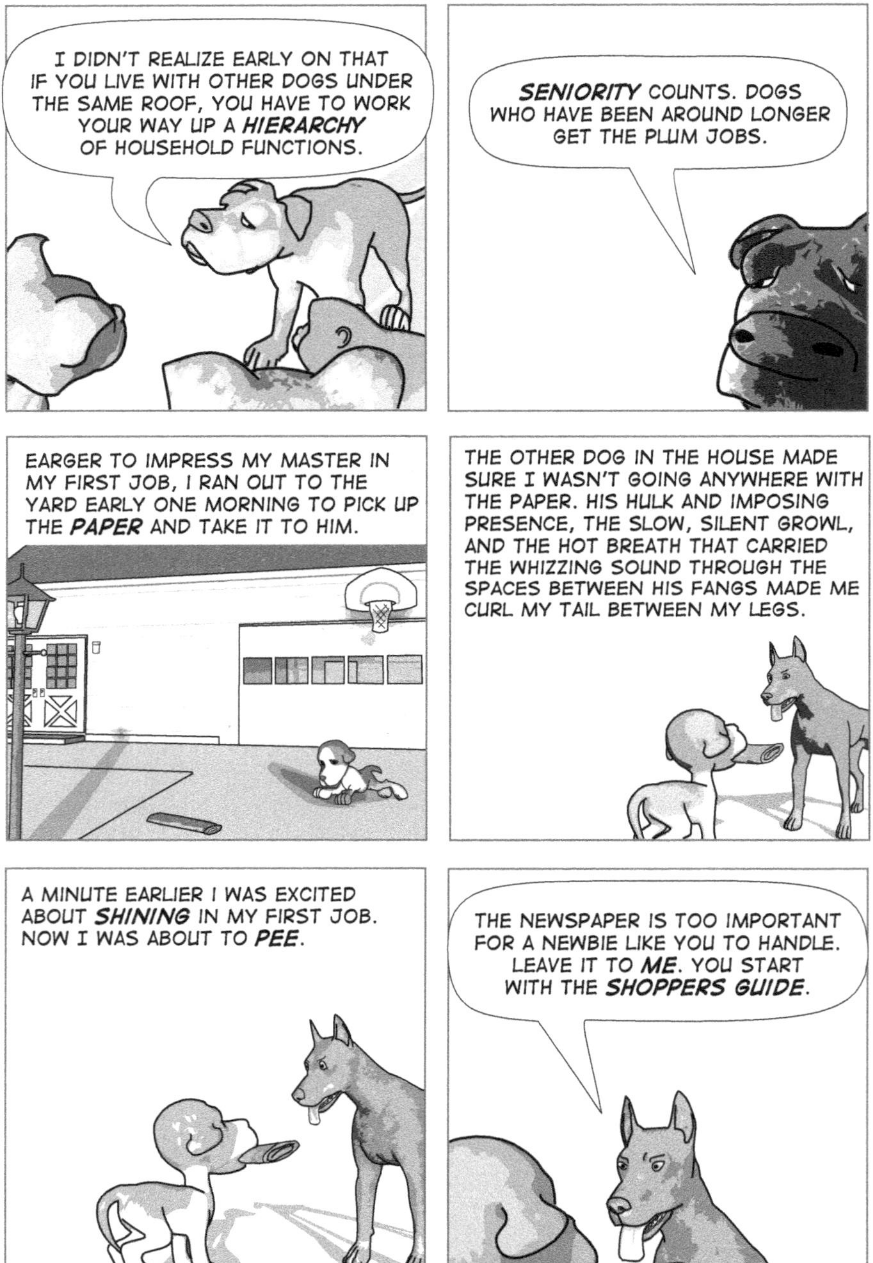
I DIDN'T REALIZE EARLY ON THAT IF YOU LIVE WITH OTHER DOGS UNDER THE SAME ROOF, YOU HAVE TO WORK YOUR WAY UP A HIERARCHY OF HOUSEHOLD FUNCTIONS.
SENIORITY COUNTS. DOGS WHO HAVE BEEN AROUND LONGER GET THE PLUM JOBS.
EARGER TO IMPRESS MY MASTER IN MY FIRST JOB, I RAN OUT TO THE YARD EARLY ONE MORNING TO PICK UP THE PAPER AND TAKE IT TO HIM.
THE OTHER DOG IN THE HOUSE MADE SURE I WASN'T GOING ANYWHERE WITH THE PAPER. HIS HULK AND IMPOSING PRESENCE, THE SLOW, SILENT GROWL, AND THE HOT BREATH THAT CARRIED THE WHIZZING SOUND THROUGH THE SPACES BETWEEN HIS FANGS MADE ME CURL MY TAIL BETWEEN MY LEGS.
A MINUTE EARLIER I WAS EXCITED ABOUT SHINING IN MY FIRST JOB. NOW I WAS ABOUT TO PEE.
THE NEWSPAPER IS TOO IMPORTANT FOR A NEWBIE LIKE YOU TO HANDLE. LEAVE IT TO ME. YOU START WITH THE SHOPPERS GUIDE.

On Writing

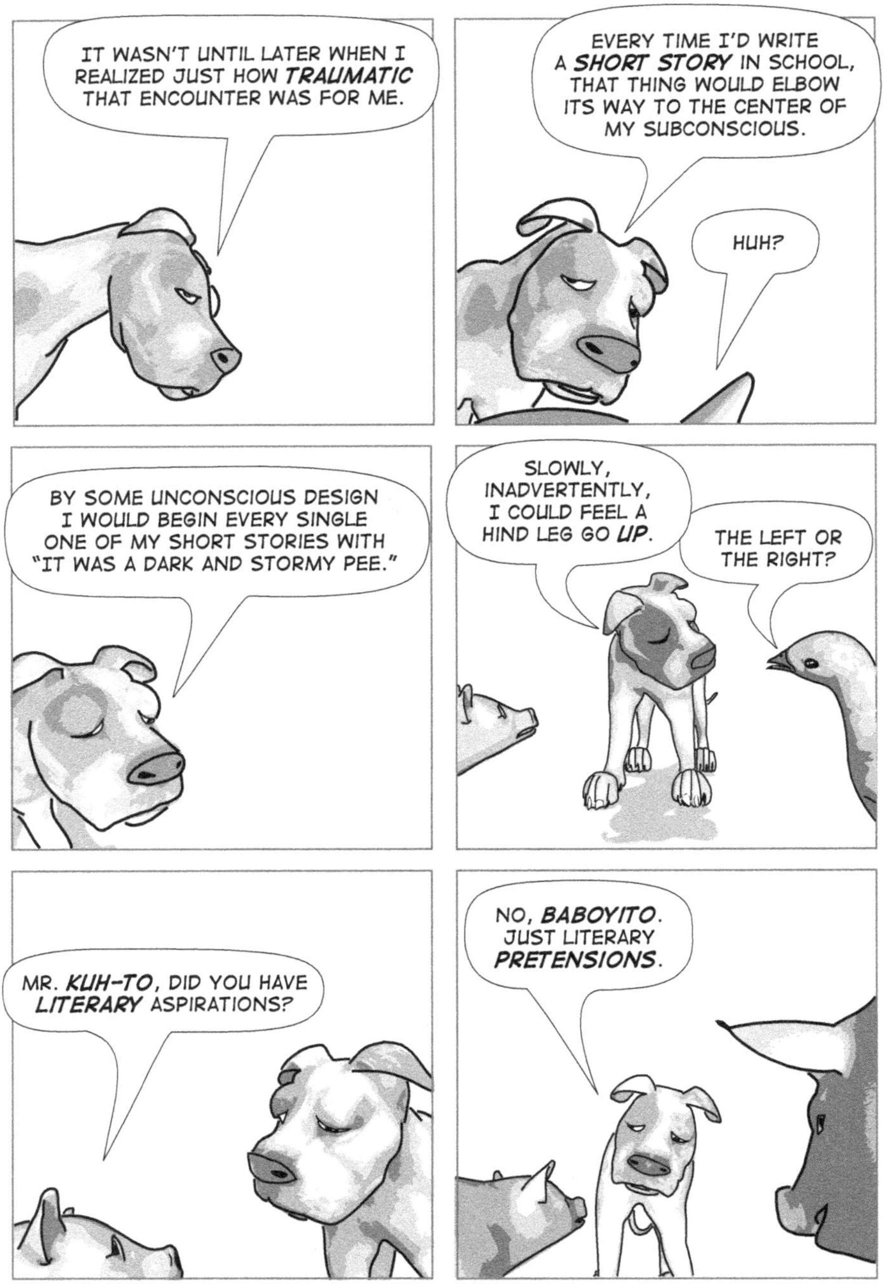
IT WASN'T UNTIL LATER WHEN I REALIZED JUST HOW ***TRAUMATIC*** THAT ENCOUNTER WAS FOR ME.
EVERY TIME I'D WRITE A ***SHORT STORY*** IN SCHOOL, THAT THING WOULD ELBOW ITS WAY TO THE CENTER OF MY SUBCONSCIOUS.
HUH?
BY SOME UNCONSCIOUS DESIGN I WOULD BEGIN EVERY SINGLE ONE OF MY SHORT STORIES WITH "IT WAS A DARK AND STORMY PEE."
SLOWLY, INADVERTENTLY, I COULD FEEL A HIND LEG GO ***UP***.
THE LEFT OR THE RIGHT?
MR. ***KUH-TO***, DID YOU HAVE ***LITERARY*** ASPIRATIONS?
NO, ***BABOYITO***. JUST LITERARY ***PRETENSIONS***.

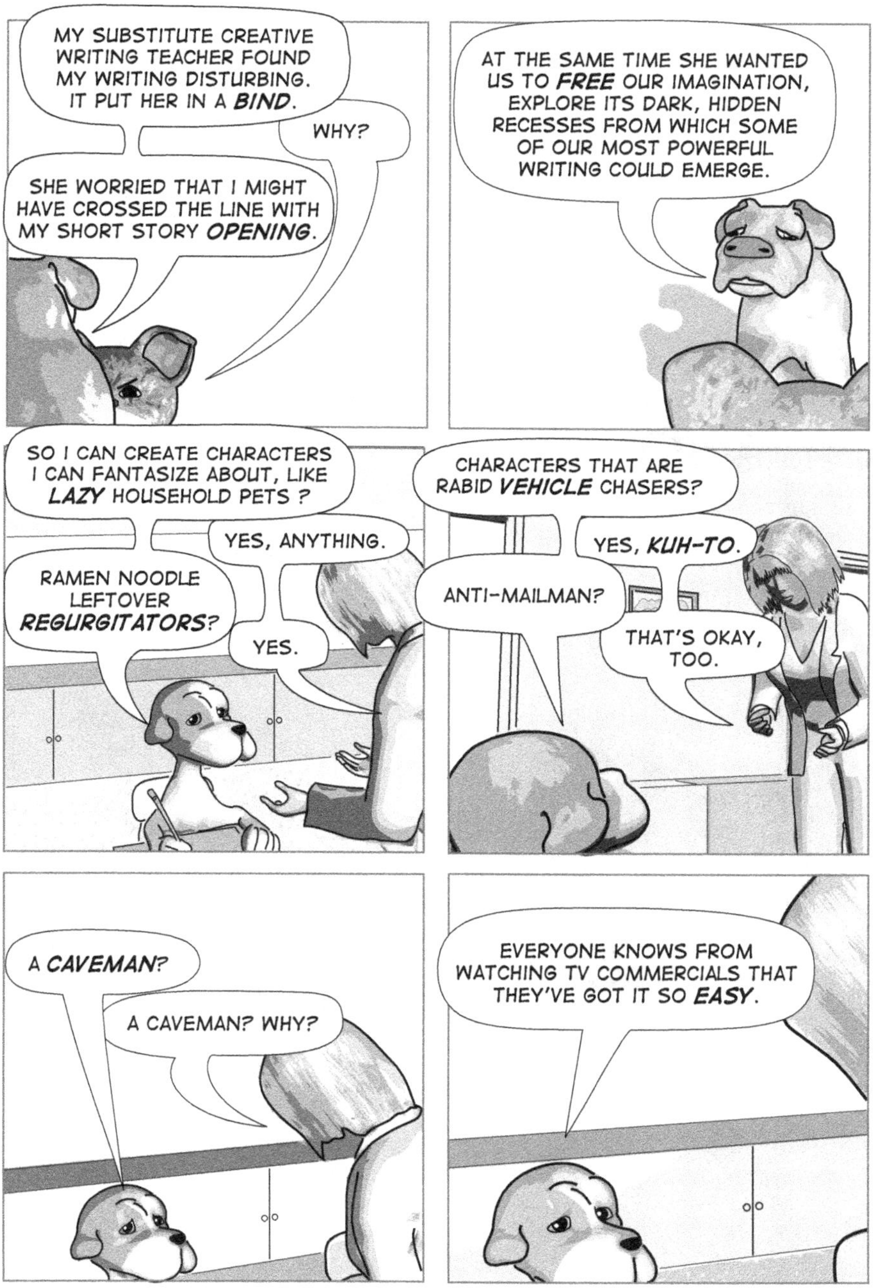
MY SUBSTITUTE CREATIVE WRITING TEACHER FOUND MY WRITING DISTURBING. IT PUT HER IN A BIND.
WHY?
SHE WORRIED THAT I MIGHT HAVE CROSSED THE LINE WITH MY SHORT STORY OPENING.
AT THE SAME TIME SHE WANTED US TO FREE OUR IMAGINATION, EXPLORE ITS DARK, HIDDEN RECESSES FROM WHICH SOME OF OUR MOST POWERFUL WRITING COULD EMERGE.
SO I CAN CREATE CHARACTERS I CAN FANTASIZE ABOUT, LIKE LAZY HOUSEHOLD PETS ?
YES, ANYTHING.
RAMEN NOODLE LEFTOVER REGURGITATORS?
YES.
CHARACTERS THAT ARE RABID VEHICLE CHASERS?
YES, KUH-TO.
ANTI-MAILMAN?
THAT'S OKAY, TOO.
A CAVEMAN?
A CAVEMAN? WHY?
EVERYONE KNOWS FROM WATCHING TV COMMERCIALS THAT THEY'VE GOT IT SO EASY.

AND A CAVEMAN IS A TRENDSETTER. EVERYTHING A CAVEMAN DOES IS A FIRST. HE STARTS A SIMPLE FIRE AND IT'S A *FIRST*.

HE FASHIONS A CLUB FROM A TREE BRANCH AND IT'S A *FIRST*.

HE HUNTS FOR FOOD AND EATS *OUT* OFTEN AND THAT'S A *FIRST*.

HE DEFENDS HIMSELF BY SWINGING HIS CLUB AT A ROCK THROWN AT HIM—

WERE YOU THINKING ABOUT THE MAKINGS OF THE VERY FIRST *BASEBALL GAME*?

110

I WAS THINKING ABOUT A KILLER PITCH . . .
. . . A BOULDER BEING ROLLED OFF A CLIFF ON THE CAVEMAN DOWN BELOW.
UH-OH. I'M GONNA NEED A BIGGER CLUB.
IT'S A FIRST FOR HIM, AND LIKELY HIS LAST.

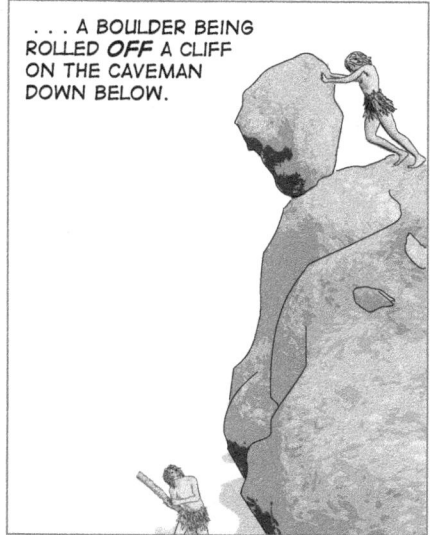

IF YOU WERE GOING FOR HUMAN CHARACTERS IN YOUR ***SHORT STORY***, WHY DIDN'T YOU GO FOR A ***FIREMAN***?
I DID, A FIREMAN WITH A ***BIG*** HOSE.
OR WHY NOT YOUR ALL-TIME FAVORITE — ***GARBAGE COLLECTOR***? DON'T TELL ME THAT SOMEHOW ESCAPED YOUR IMAGINATION.
I ***DIDN'T*** THINK THAT WAS GOOD ENOUGH.
ALL THE SAND ON THE BEACH AND YOU DON'T HAVE ENOUGH FOR A SANDCASTLE?
I WENT HIGHER UP THE HIERARCHY—***WASTE*** MANAGEMENT DIRECTOR.

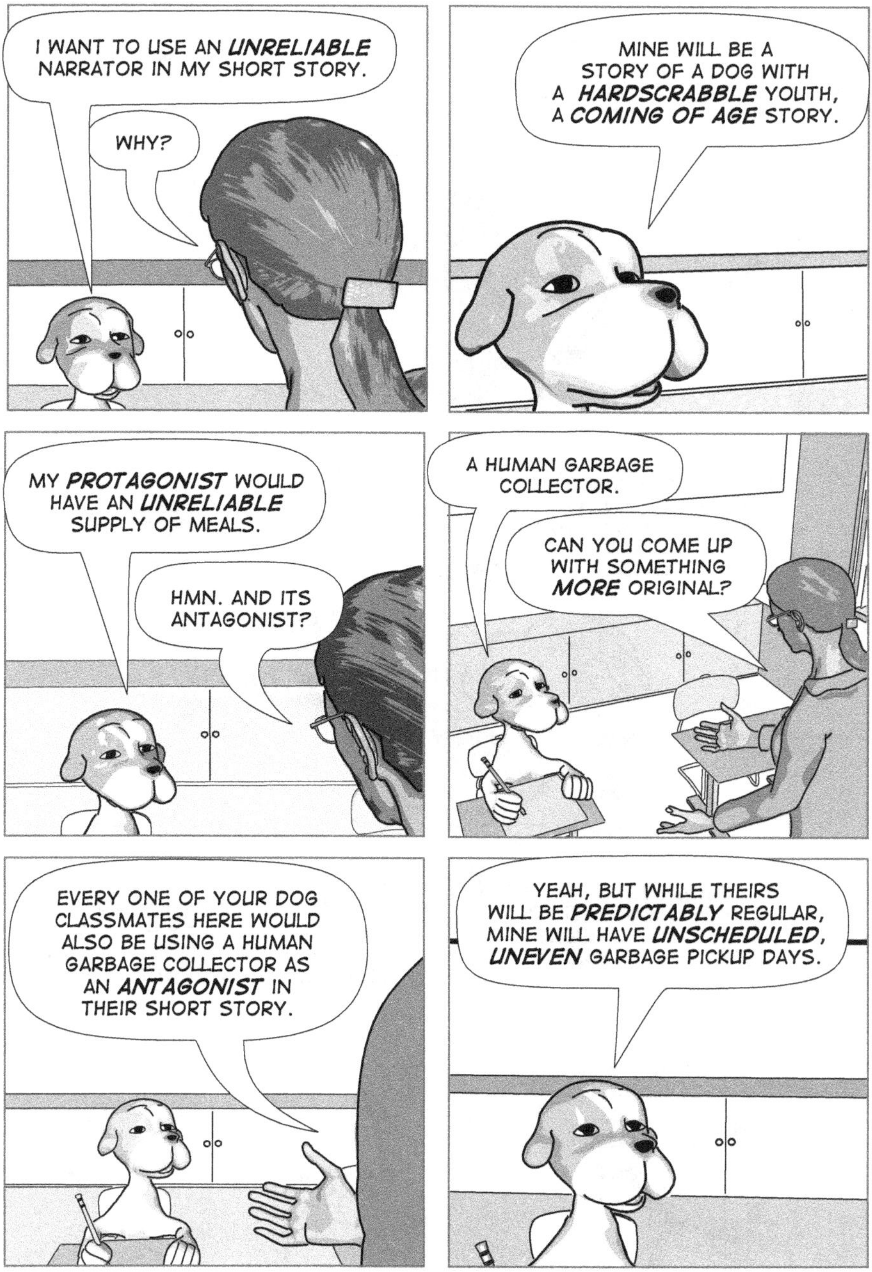
I WANT TO USE AN UNRELIABLE NARRATOR IN MY SHORT STORY.
WHY?
MINE WILL BE A STORY OF A DOG WITH A HARDSCRABBLE YOUTH, A COMING OF AGE STORY.
MY PROTAGONIST WOULD HAVE AN UNRELIABLE SUPPLY OF MEALS.
HMN. AND ITS ANTAGONIST?
A HUMAN GARBAGE COLLECTOR.
CAN YOU COME UP WITH SOMETHING MORE ORIGINAL?
EVERY ONE OF YOUR DOG CLASSMATES HERE WOULD ALSO BE USING A HUMAN GARBAGE COLLECTOR AS AN ANTAGONIST IN THEIR SHORT STORY.
YEAH, BUT WHILE THEIRS WILL BE PREDICTABLY REGULAR, MINE WILL HAVE UNSCHEDULED, UNEVEN GARBAGE PICKUP DAYS.

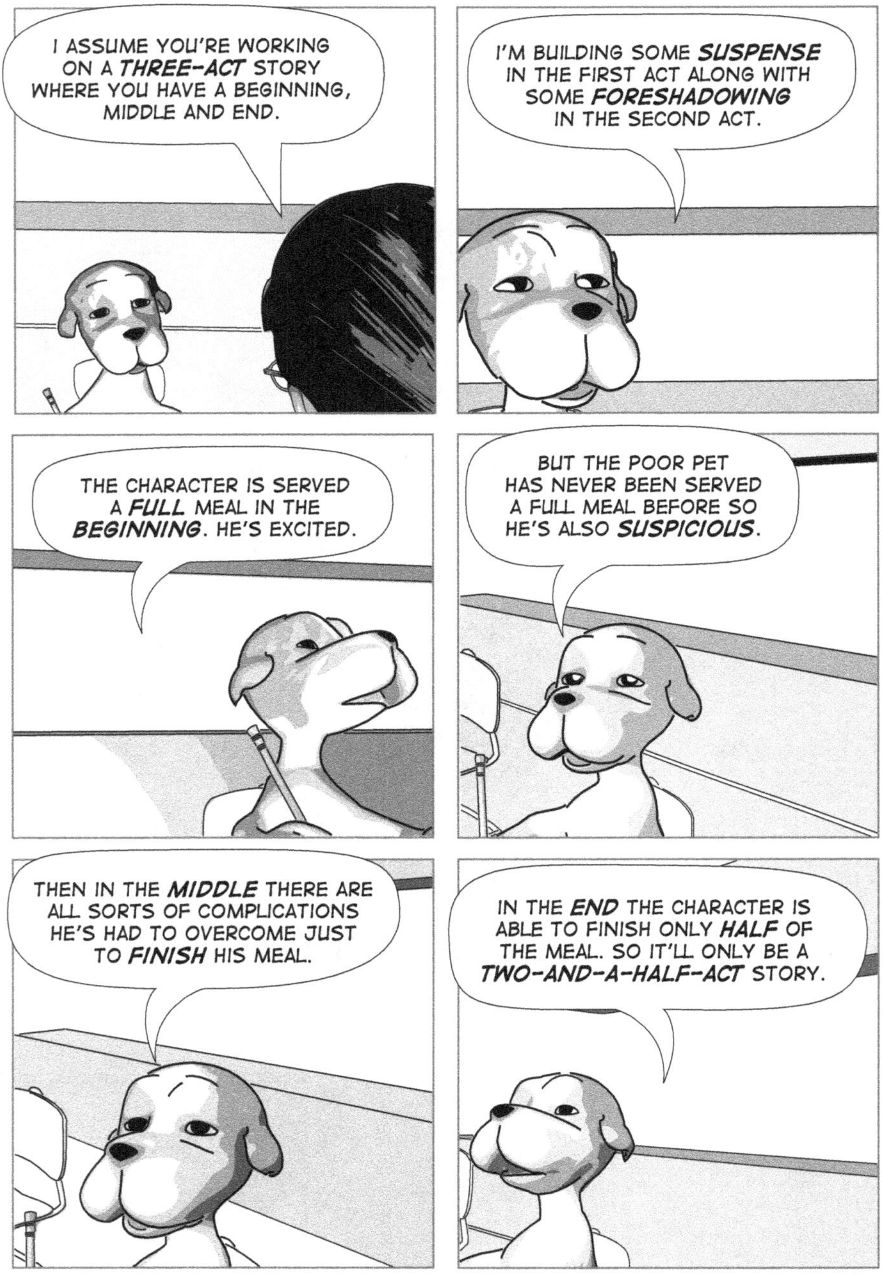
I ASSUME YOU'RE WORKING ON A *THREE-ACT* STORY WHERE YOU HAVE A BEGINNING, MIDDLE AND END.
I'M BUILDING SOME *SUSPENSE* IN THE FIRST ACT ALONG WITH SOME *FORESHADOWING* IN THE SECOND ACT.
THE CHARACTER IS SERVED A *FULL* MEAL IN THE *BEGINNING*. HE'S EXCITED.
BUT THE POOR PET HAS NEVER BEEN SERVED A FULL MEAL BEFORE SO HE'S ALSO *SUSPICIOUS*.
THEN IN THE *MIDDLE* THERE ARE ALL SORTS OF COMPLICATIONS HE'S HAD TO OVERCOME JUST TO *FINISH* HIS MEAL.
IN THE *END* THE CHARACTER IS ABLE TO FINISH ONLY *HALF* OF THE MEAL. SO IT'LL ONLY BE A *TWO-AND-A-HALF-ACT* STORY.

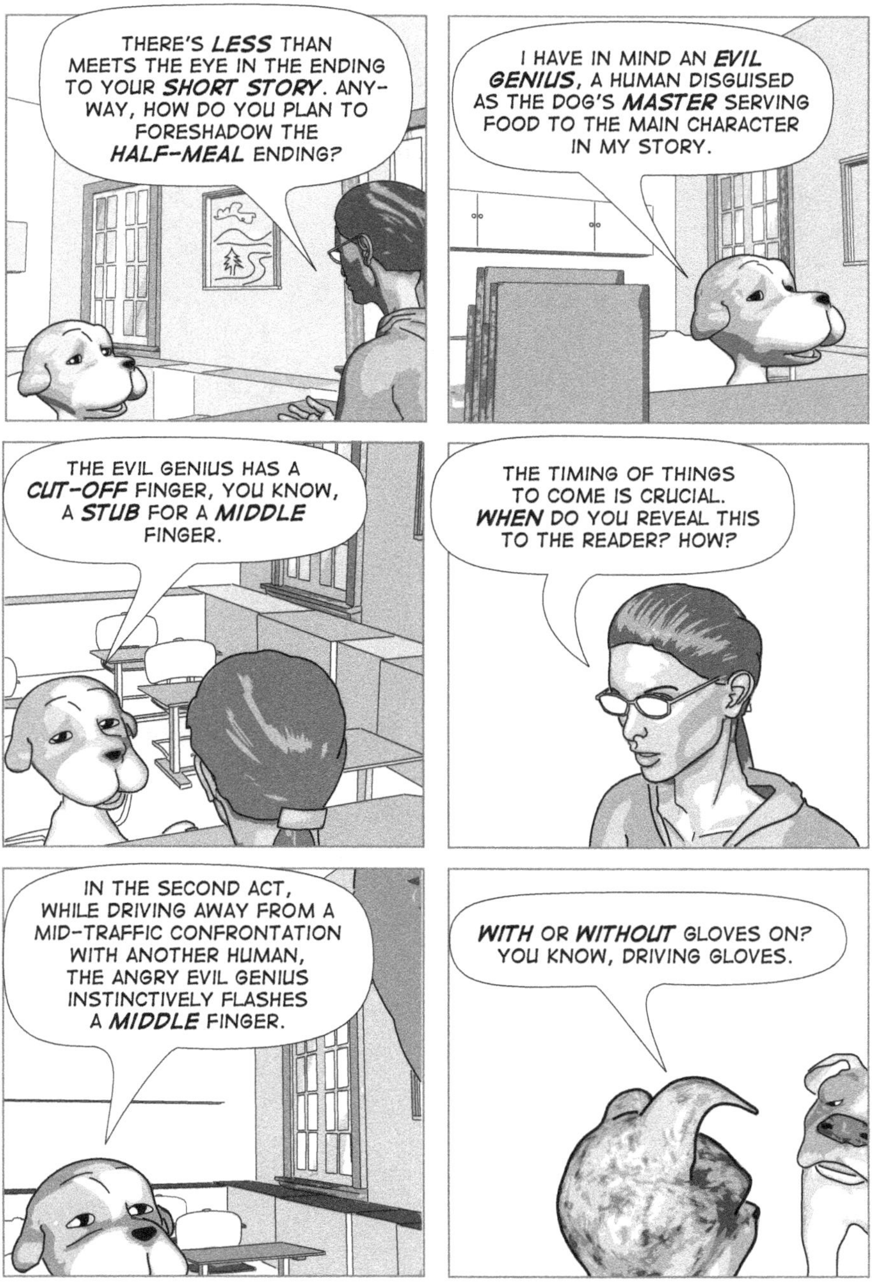
THERE'S LESS THAN MEETS THE EYE IN THE ENDING TO YOUR SHORT STORY. ANY-WAY, HOW DO YOU PLAN TO FORESHADOW THE HALF-MEAL ENDING?
I HAVE IN MIND AN EVIL GENIUS, A HUMAN DISGUISED AS THE DOG'S MASTER SERVING FOOD TO THE MAIN CHARACTER IN MY STORY.
THE EVIL GENIUS HAS A CUT-OFF FINGER, YOU KNOW, A STUB FOR A MIDDLE FINGER.
THE TIMING OF THINGS TO COME IS CRUCIAL. WHEN DO YOU REVEAL THIS TO THE READER? HOW?
IN THE SECOND ACT, WHILE DRIVING AWAY FROM A MID-TRAFFIC CONFRONTATION WITH ANOTHER HUMAN, THE ANGRY EVIL GENIUS INSTINCTIVELY FLASHES A MIDDLE FINGER.
WITH OR WITHOUT GLOVES ON? YOU KNOW, DRIVING GLOVES.

Granny Wants to Go to America

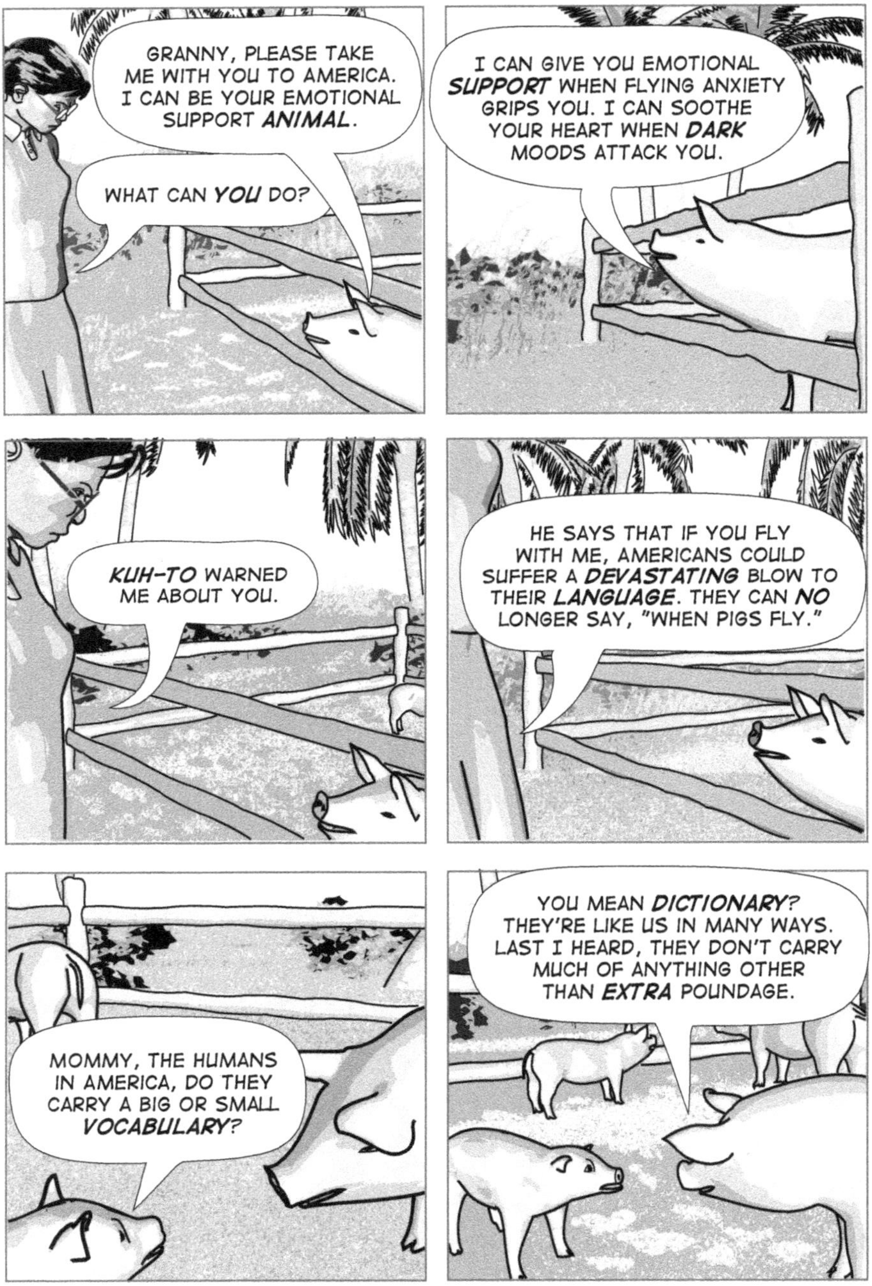
GRANNY, PLEASE TAKE ME WITH YOU TO AMERICA. I CAN BE YOUR EMOTIONAL SUPPORT ANIMAL.
WHAT CAN YOU DO?
I CAN GIVE YOU EMOTIONAL SUPPORT WHEN FLYING ANXIETY GRIPS YOU. I CAN SOOTHE YOUR HEART WHEN DARK MOODS ATTACK YOU.
KUH-TO WARNED ME ABOUT YOU.
HE SAYS THAT IF YOU FLY WITH ME, AMERICANS COULD SUFFER A DEVASTATING BLOW TO THEIR LANGUAGE. THEY CAN NO LONGER SAY, "WHEN PIGS FLY."
MOMMY, THE HUMANS IN AMERICA, DO THEY CARRY A BIG OR SMALL VOCABULARY?
YOU MEAN DICTIONARY? THEY'RE LIKE US IN MANY WAYS. LAST I HEARD, THEY DON'T CARRY MUCH OF ANYTHING OTHER THAN EXTRA POUNDAGE.

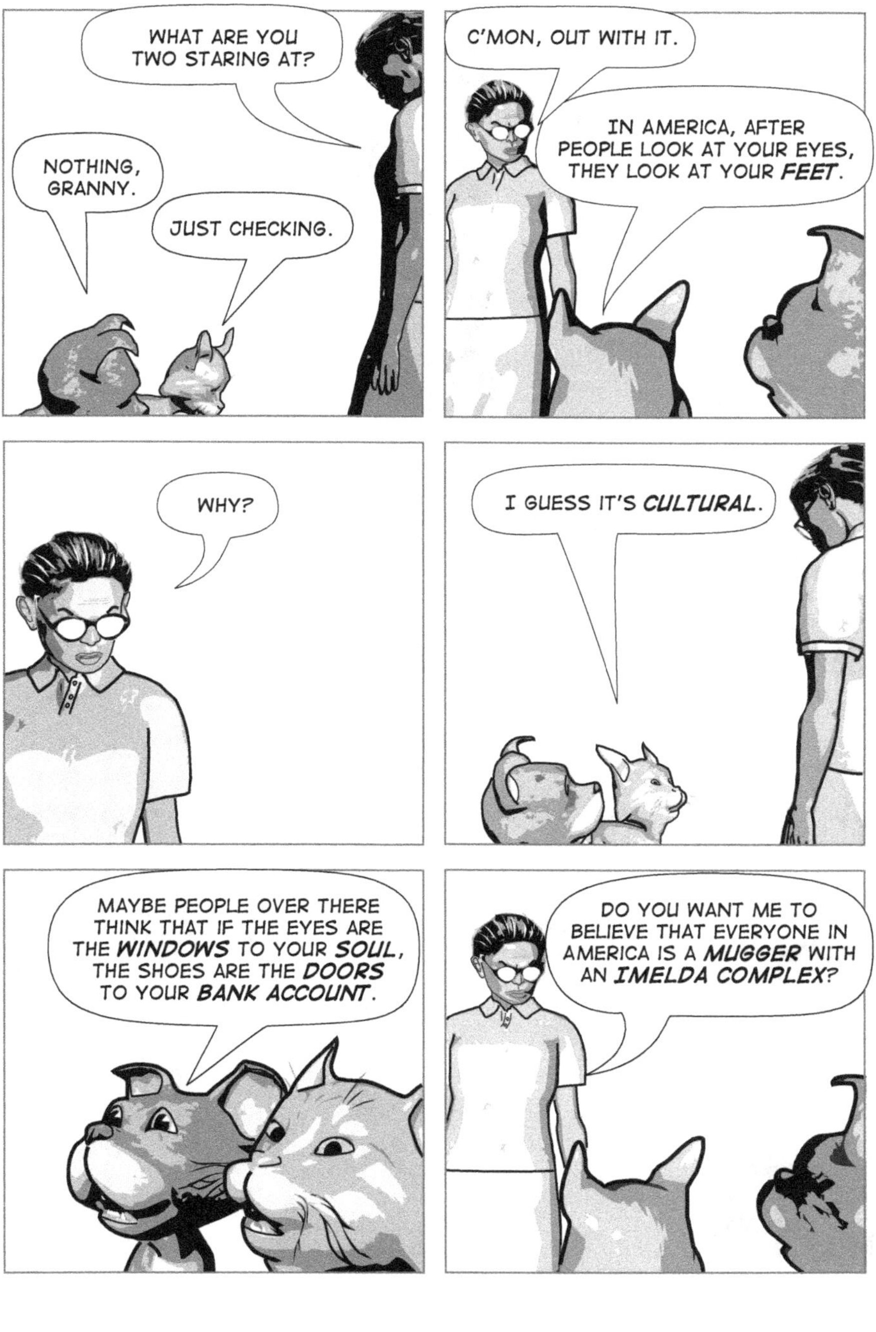
WHAT ARE YOU TWO STARING AT?
NOTHING, GRANNY.
JUST CHECKING.
C'MON, OUT WITH IT.
IN AMERICA, AFTER PEOPLE LOOK AT YOUR EYES, THEY LOOK AT YOUR *FEET*.
WHY?
I GUESS IT'S *CULTURAL*.
MAYBE PEOPLE OVER THERE THINK THAT IF THE EYES ARE THE *WINDOWS* TO YOUR *SOUL*, THE SHOES ARE THE *DOORS* TO YOUR *BANK ACCOUNT*.
DO YOU WANT ME TO BELIEVE THAT EVERYONE IN AMERICA IS A *MUGGER* WITH AN *IMELDA COMPLEX*?

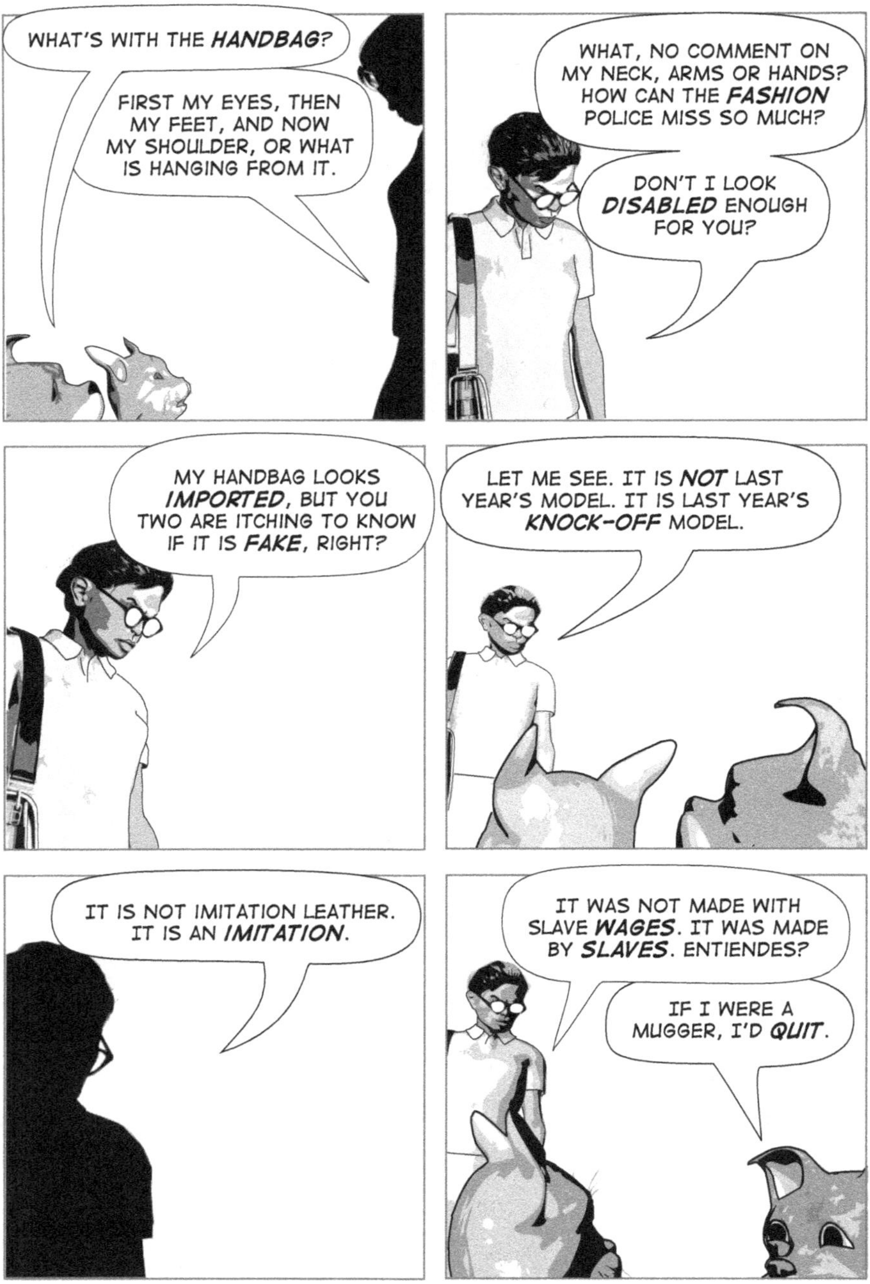
WHAT'S WITH THE *HANDBAG*?
FIRST MY EYES, THEN MY FEET, AND NOW MY SHOULDER, OR WHAT IS HANGING FROM IT.
WHAT, NO COMMENT ON MY NECK, ARMS OR HANDS? HOW CAN THE *FASHION* POLICE MISS SO MUCH?
DON'T I LOOK *DISABLED* ENOUGH FOR YOU?
MY HANDBAG LOOKS *IMPORTED*, BUT YOU TWO ARE ITCHING TO KNOW IF IT IS *FAKE*, RIGHT?
LET ME SEE. IT IS *NOT* LAST YEAR'S MODEL. IT IS LAST YEAR'S *KNOCK-OFF* MODEL.
IT IS NOT IMITATION LEATHER. IT IS AN *IMITATION*.
IT WAS NOT MADE WITH SLAVE *WAGES*. IT WAS MADE BY *SLAVES*. ENTIENDES?
IF I WERE A MUGGER, I'D *QUIT*.

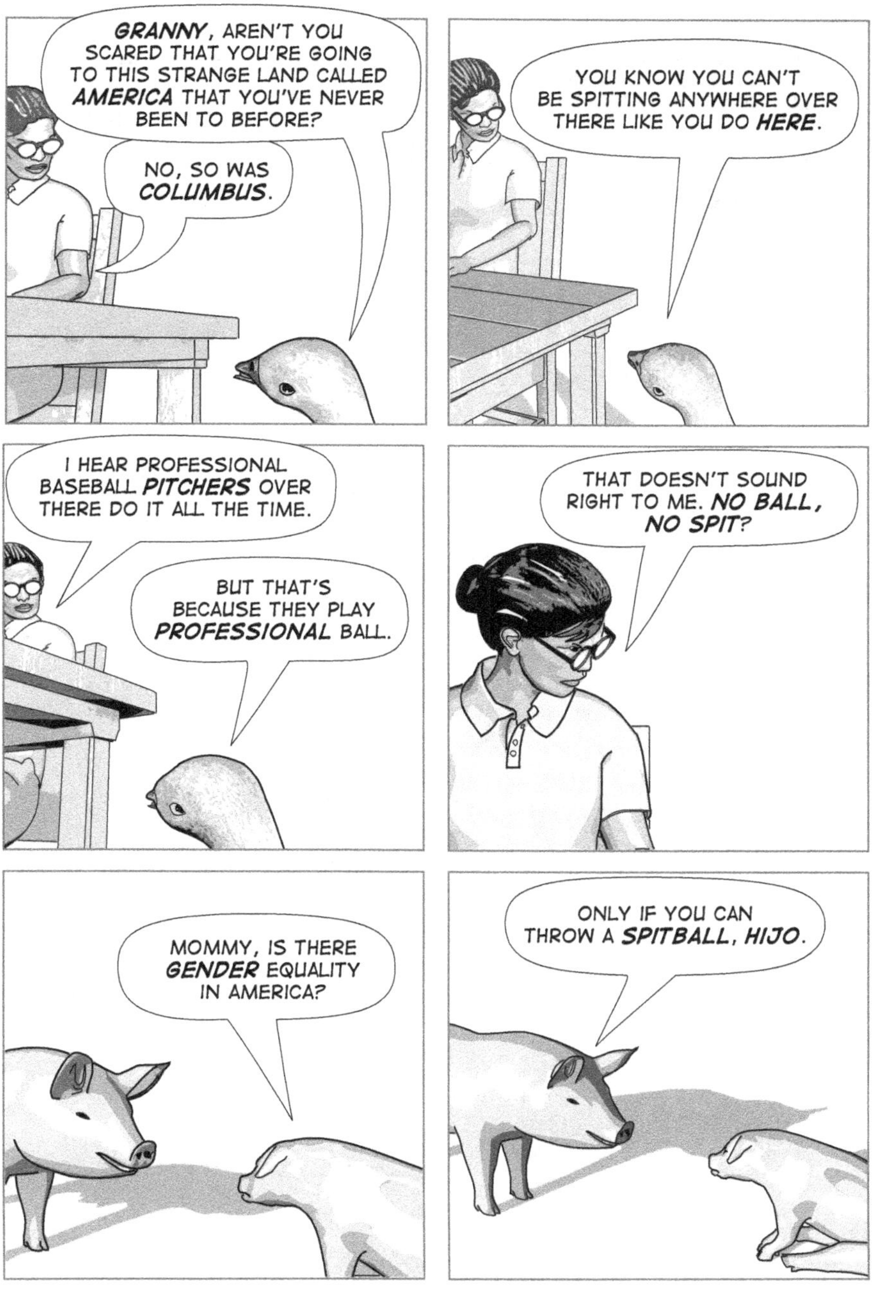
GRANNY, AREN'T YOU SCARED THAT YOU'RE GOING TO THIS STRANGE LAND CALLED AMERICA THAT YOU'VE NEVER BEEN TO BEFORE?
NO, SO WAS COLUMBUS.
YOU KNOW YOU CAN'T BE SPITTING ANYWHERE OVER THERE LIKE YOU DO HERE.
I HEAR PROFESSIONAL BASEBALL PITCHERS OVER THERE DO IT ALL THE TIME.
BUT THAT'S BECAUSE THEY PLAY PROFESSIONAL BALL.
THAT DOESN'T SOUND RIGHT TO ME. NO BALL, NO SPIT?
MOMMY, IS THERE GENDER EQUALITY IN AMERICA?
ONLY IF YOU CAN THROW A SPITBALL, HIJO.

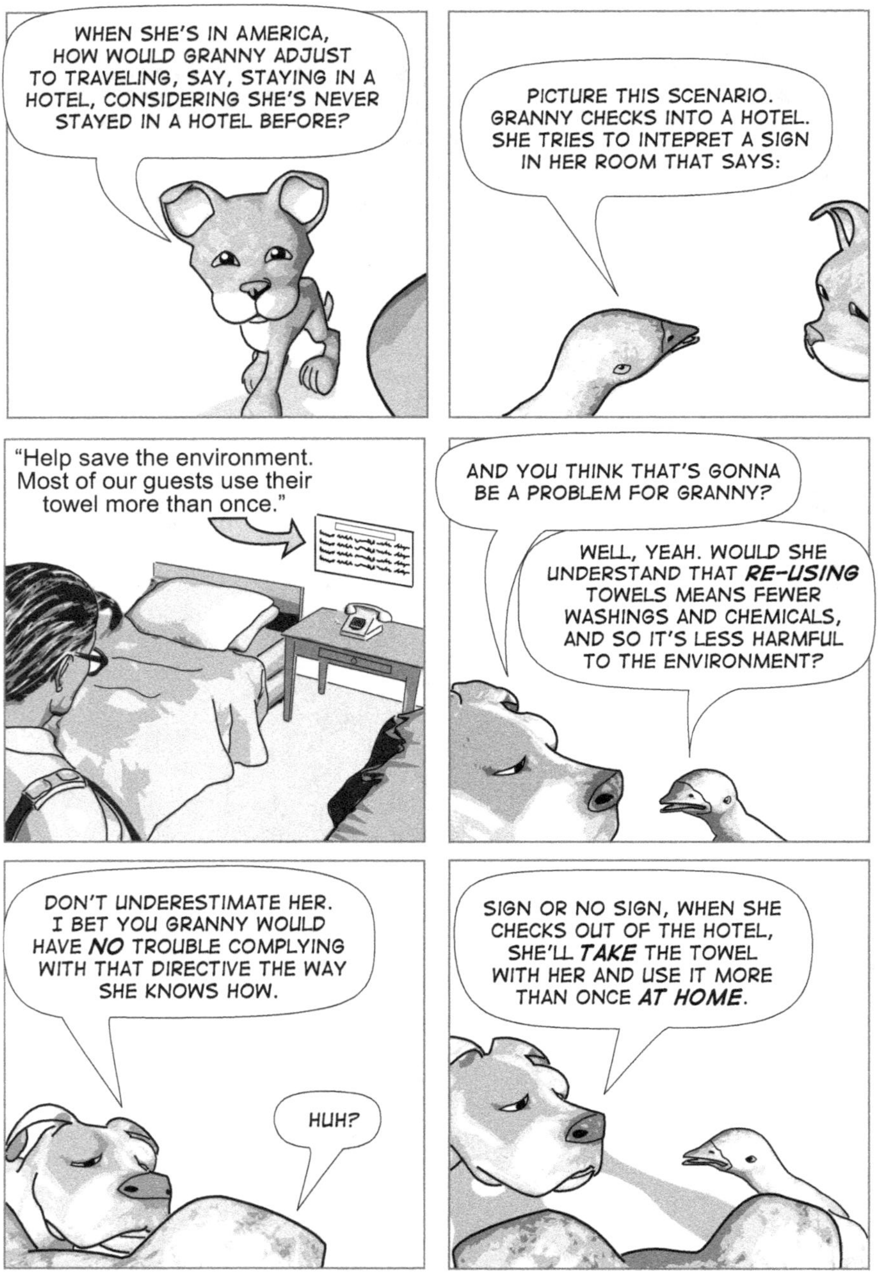
WHEN SHE'S IN AMERICA, HOW WOULD GRANNY ADJUST TO TRAVELING, SAY, STAYING IN A HOTEL, CONSIDERING SHE'S NEVER STAYED IN A HOTEL BEFORE?
PICTURE THIS SCENARIO. GRANNY CHECKS INTO A HOTEL. SHE TRIES TO INTEPRET A SIGN IN HER ROOM THAT SAYS:
"Help save the environment. Most of our guests use their towel more than once."
AND YOU THINK THAT'S GONNA BE A PROBLEM FOR GRANNY?
WELL, YEAH. WOULD SHE UNDERSTAND THAT *RE-USING* TOWELS MEANS FEWER WASHINGS AND CHEMICALS, AND SO IT'S LESS HARMFUL TO THE ENVIRONMENT?
DON'T UNDERESTIMATE HER. I BET YOU GRANNY WOULD HAVE *NO* TROUBLE COMPLYING WITH THAT DIRECTIVE THE WAY SHE KNOWS HOW.
HUH?
SIGN OR NO SIGN, WHEN SHE CHECKS OUT OF THE HOTEL, SHE'LL *TAKE* THE TOWEL WITH HER AND USE IT MORE THAN ONCE *AT HOME*.

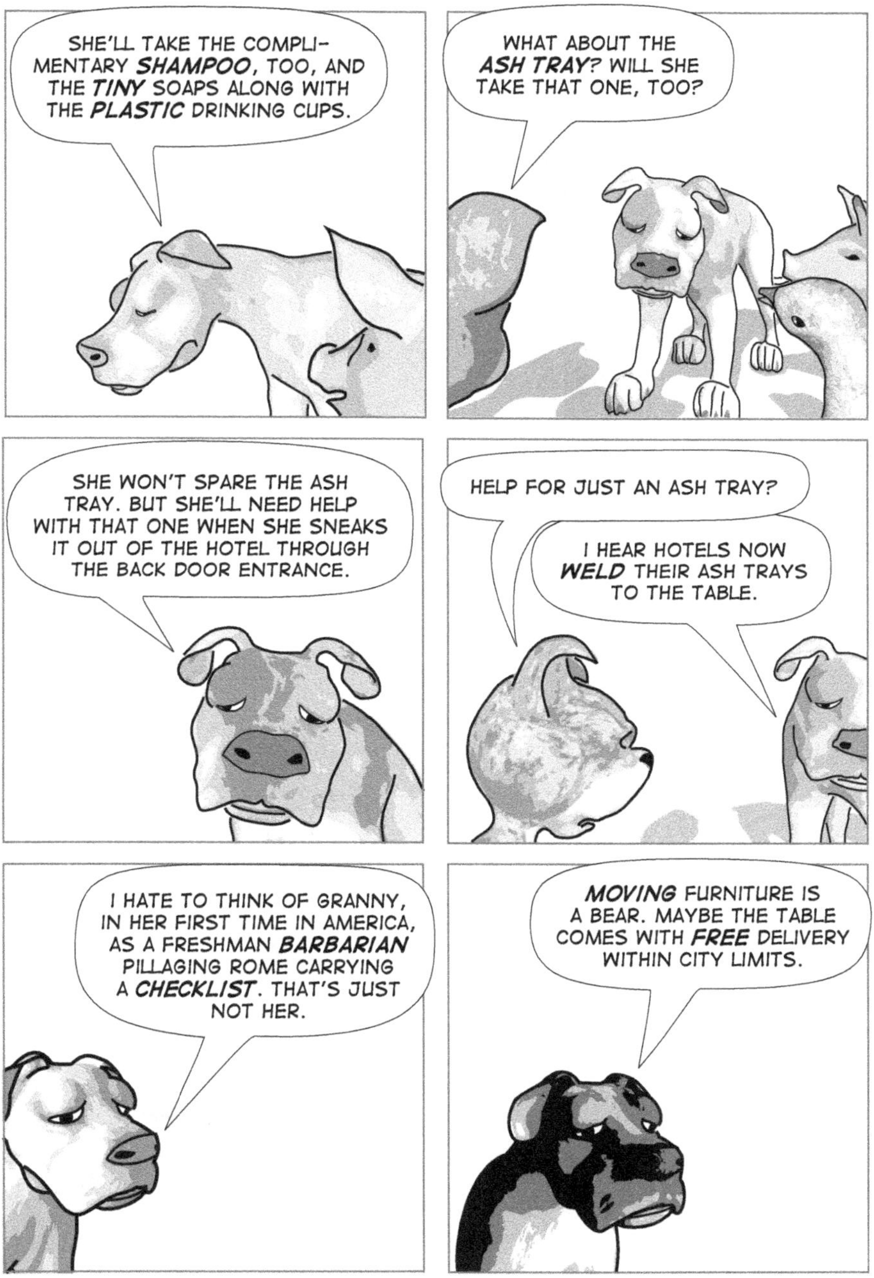
SHE'LL TAKE THE COMPLI-MENTARY SHAMPOO, TOO, AND THE TINY SOAPS ALONG WITH THE PLASTIC DRINKING CUPS.
WHAT ABOUT THE ASH TRAY? WILL SHE TAKE THAT ONE, TOO?
SHE WON'T SPARE THE ASH TRAY. BUT SHE'LL NEED HELP WITH THAT ONE WHEN SHE SNEAKS IT OUT OF THE HOTEL THROUGH THE BACK DOOR ENTRANCE.
HELP FOR JUST AN ASH TRAY?
I HEAR HOTELS NOW WELD THEIR ASH TRAYS TO THE TABLE.
I HATE TO THINK OF GRANNY, IN HER FIRST TIME IN AMERICA, AS A FRESHMAN BARBARIAN PILLAGING ROME CARRYING A CHECKLIST. THAT'S JUST NOT HER.
MOVING FURNITURE IS A BEAR. MAYBE THE TABLE COMES WITH FREE DELIVERY WITHIN CITY LIMITS.

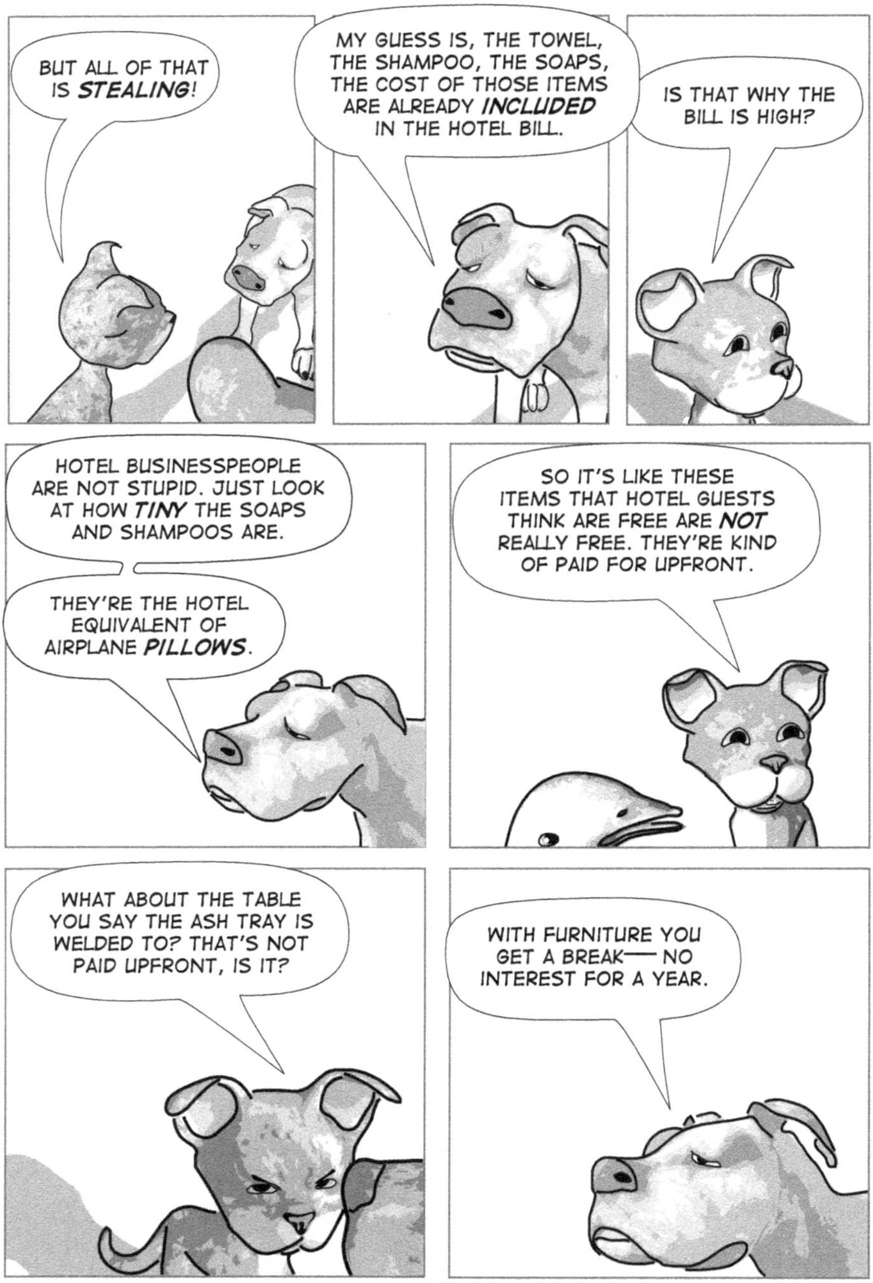
BUT ALL OF THAT IS STEALING!
MY GUESS IS, THE TOWEL, THE SHAMPOO, THE SOAPS, THE COST OF THOSE ITEMS ARE ALREADY INCLUDED IN THE HOTEL BILL.
IS THAT WHY THE BILL IS HIGH?
HOTEL BUSINESSPEOPLE ARE NOT STUPID. JUST LOOK AT HOW TINY THE SOAPS AND SHAMPOOS ARE.
THEY'RE THE HOTEL EQUIVALENT OF AIRPLANE PILLOWS.
SO IT'S LIKE THESE ITEMS THAT HOTEL GUESTS THINK ARE FREE ARE NOT REALLY FREE. THEY'RE KIND OF PAID FOR UPFRONT.
WHAT ABOUT THE TABLE YOU SAY THE ASH TRAY IS WELDED TO? THAT'S NOT PAID UPFRONT, IS IT?
WITH FURNITURE YOU GET A BREAK— NO INTEREST FOR A YEAR.

BY EXTENSION, IF GRANNY DOES ENOUGH TRAVELING ACROSS AMERICA, THEN YOU'D FIND IN HER HOME WHAT YOU'D FIND IN A CHEAP HOTEL.
MY QUESTION IS: WOULD HER FRIENDS STILL WANT TO VISIT HER AT HOME?
I DON'T SEE THE POINT.
WHY WOULD YOU WANT TO SLEEP OVER AT A FRIEND'S HOUSE WHERE YOU'RE MADE TO FEEL LIKE YOU'RE STAYING IN A CHEAP HOTEL?
YOU KNOW, THE TINY SOAP BAR, THE MEAGER SHAMPOO.
IF YOU DON'T HAVE CABLE TV AT HOME, WHO CARES IF YOU WASHED OR SHAMPOOED ENOUGH? I DON'T.

Masters of All Stripes

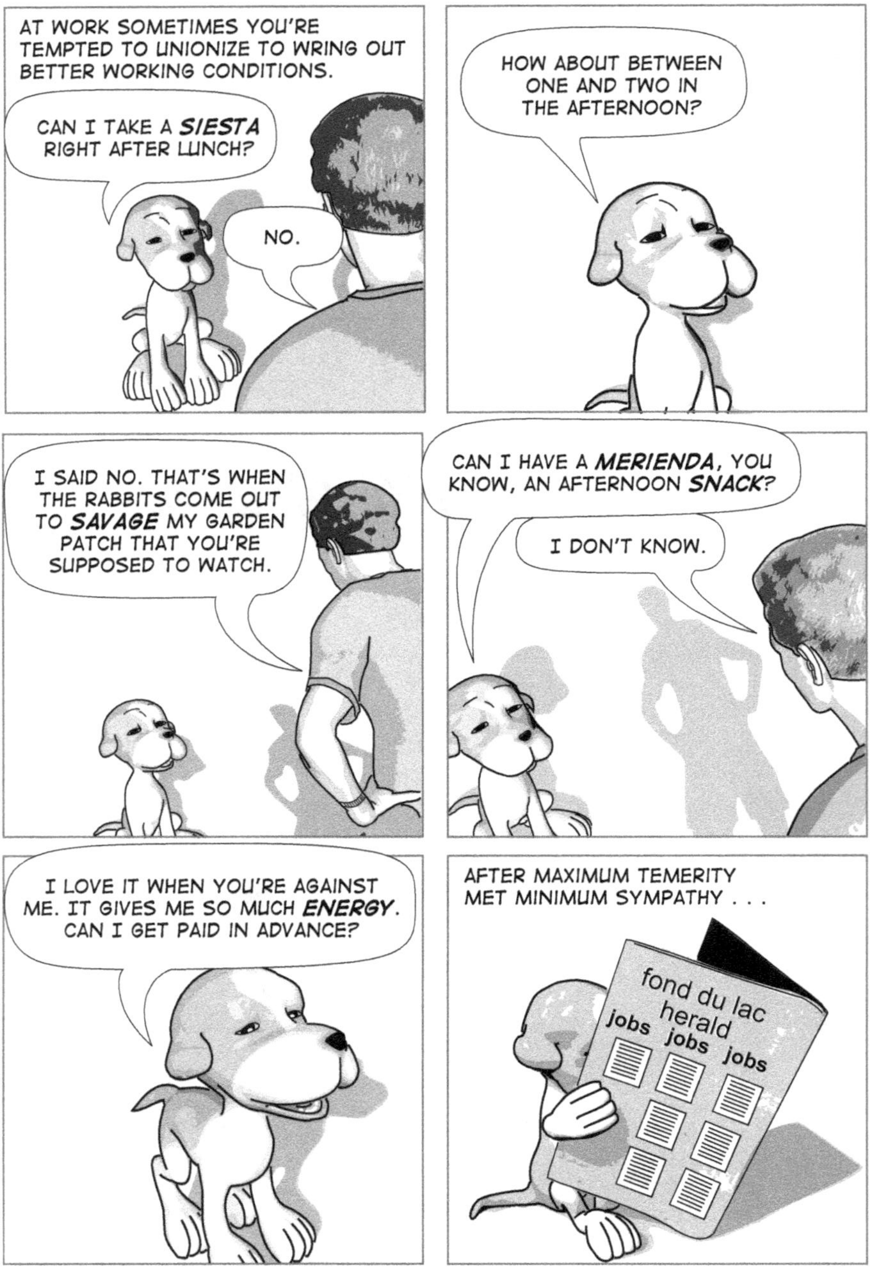
AT WORK SOMETIMES YOU'RE TEMPTED TO UNIONIZE TO WRING OUT BETTER WORKING CONDITIONS.
CAN I TAKE A ***SIESTA*** RIGHT AFTER LUNCH?
NO.
HOW ABOUT BETWEEN ONE AND TWO IN THE AFTERNOON?
I SAID NO. THAT'S WHEN THE RABBITS COME OUT TO ***SAVAGE*** MY GARDEN PATCH THAT YOU'RE SUPPOSED TO WATCH.
CAN I HAVE A ***MERIENDA***, YOU KNOW, AN AFTERNOON ***SNACK***?
I DON'T KNOW.
I LOVE IT WHEN YOU'RE AGAINST ME. IT GIVES ME SO MUCH ***ENERGY***. CAN I GET PAID IN ADVANCE?
AFTER MAXIMUM TEMERITY MET MINIMUM SYMPATHY . . .
fond du lac herald
jobs jobs jobs

MR. *KUH-TO*, HAVE YOU EVER HAD AN *IMMIGRANT* MASTER WHO HAD SORT OF MADE IT *BIG* IN AMERICA?
THE *GOOD* NEWS ABOUT WORKING FOR SUCCESSFUL IMMIGRANT MASTERS IS THEY SHARE YOUR VALUES AND "SENTIMIENTOS."
THEY INSPIRE YOU AND YOU IN TURN INSPIRE THEM. YOU REMIND THEM OF THEIR EARLY STRUGGLES IN AMERICA.
AND THE BAD NEWS?
THE BAD NEWS IS WHEN *YOU* START SHARING WITH THEM THOSE VERY SAME VALUES AND "SENTIMIENTOS" THAT MADE YOUR IMMIGRANT MASTERS SUCCESSFUL.
THEY DON'T LIKE IT WHEN YOU *HAGGLE* OVER PAY.

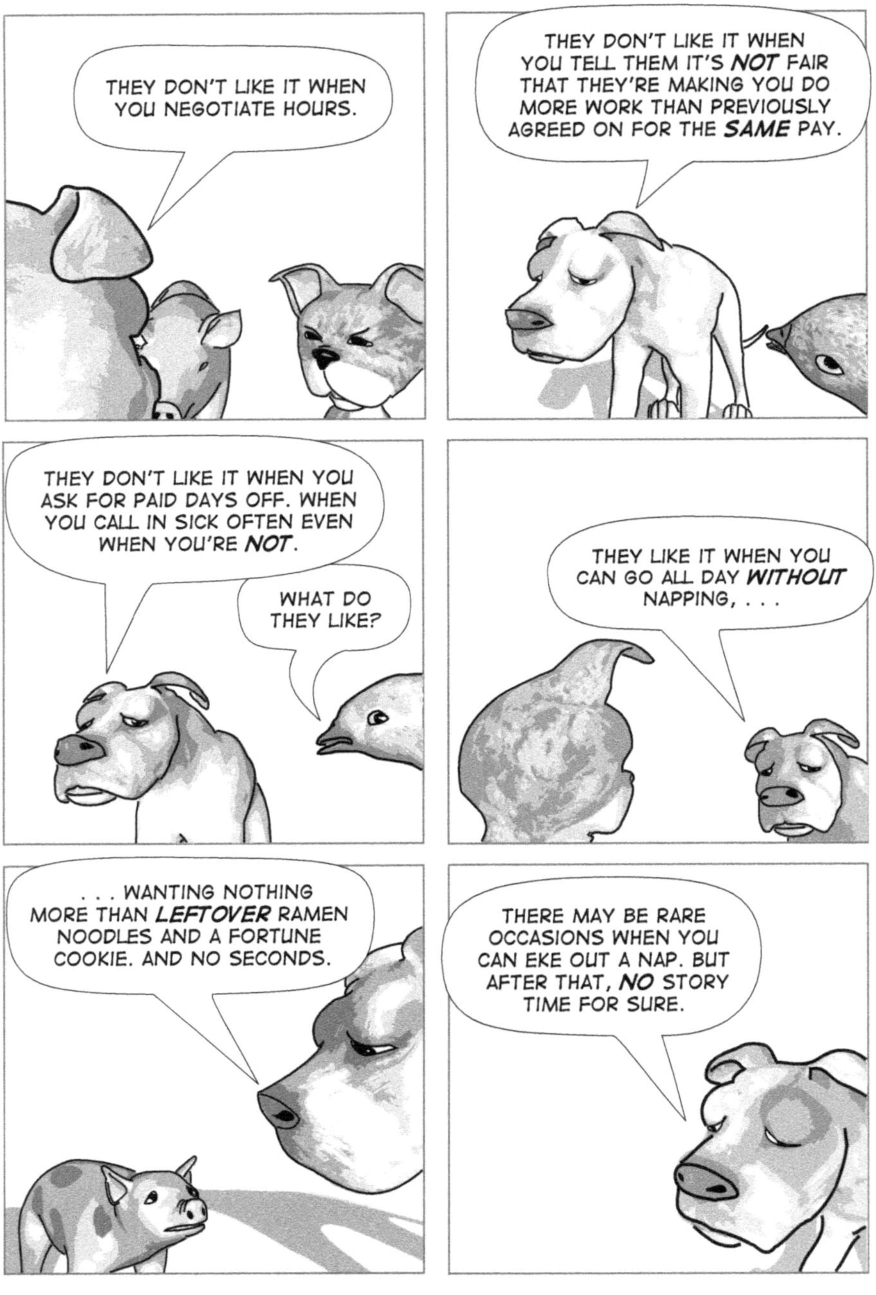
THEY DON'T LIKE IT WHEN YOU NEGOTIATE HOURS.
THEY DON'T LIKE IT WHEN YOU TELL THEM IT'S *NOT* FAIR THAT THEY'RE MAKING YOU DO MORE WORK THAN PREVIOUSLY AGREED ON FOR THE *SAME* PAY.
THEY DON'T LIKE IT WHEN YOU ASK FOR PAID DAYS OFF. WHEN YOU CALL IN SICK OFTEN EVEN WHEN YOU'RE *NOT*.
WHAT DO THEY LIKE?
THEY LIKE IT WHEN YOU CAN GO ALL DAY *WITHOUT* NAPPING, . . .
. . . WANTING NOTHING MORE THAN *LEFTOVER* RAMEN NOODLES AND A FORTUNE COOKIE. AND NO SECONDS.
THERE MAY BE RARE OCCASIONS WHEN YOU CAN EKE OUT A NAP. BUT AFTER THAT, *NO* STORY TIME FOR SURE.

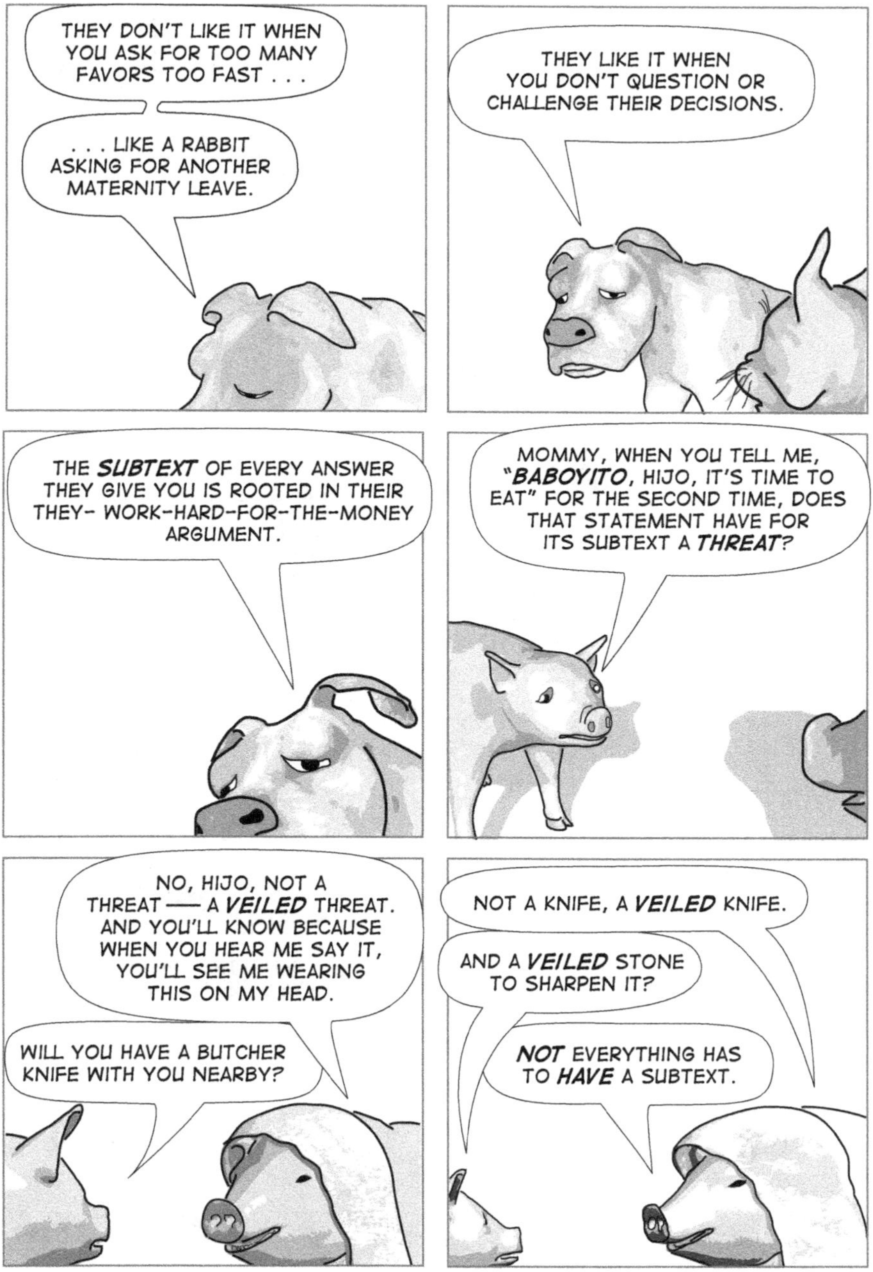
THEY DON'T LIKE IT WHEN YOU ASK FOR TOO MANY FAVORS TOO FAST . . .
. . . LIKE A RABBIT ASKING FOR ANOTHER MATERNITY LEAVE.
THEY LIKE IT WHEN YOU DON'T QUESTION OR CHALLENGE THEIR DECISIONS.
THE *SUBTEXT* OF EVERY ANSWER THEY GIVE YOU IS ROOTED IN THEIR THEY- WORK-HARD-FOR-THE-MONEY ARGUMENT.
MOMMY, WHEN YOU TELL ME, "*BABOYITO*, HIJO, IT'S TIME TO EAT" FOR THE SECOND TIME, DOES THAT STATEMENT HAVE FOR ITS SUBTEXT A *THREAT*?
NO, HIJO, NOT A THREAT — A *VEILED* THREAT. AND YOU'LL KNOW BECAUSE WHEN YOU HEAR ME SAY IT, YOU'LL SEE ME WEARING THIS ON MY HEAD.
WILL YOU HAVE A BUTCHER KNIFE WITH YOU NEARBY?
NOT A KNIFE, A *VEILED* KNIFE.
AND A *VEILED* STONE TO SHARPEN IT?
NOT EVERYTHING HAS TO *HAVE* A SUBTEXT.

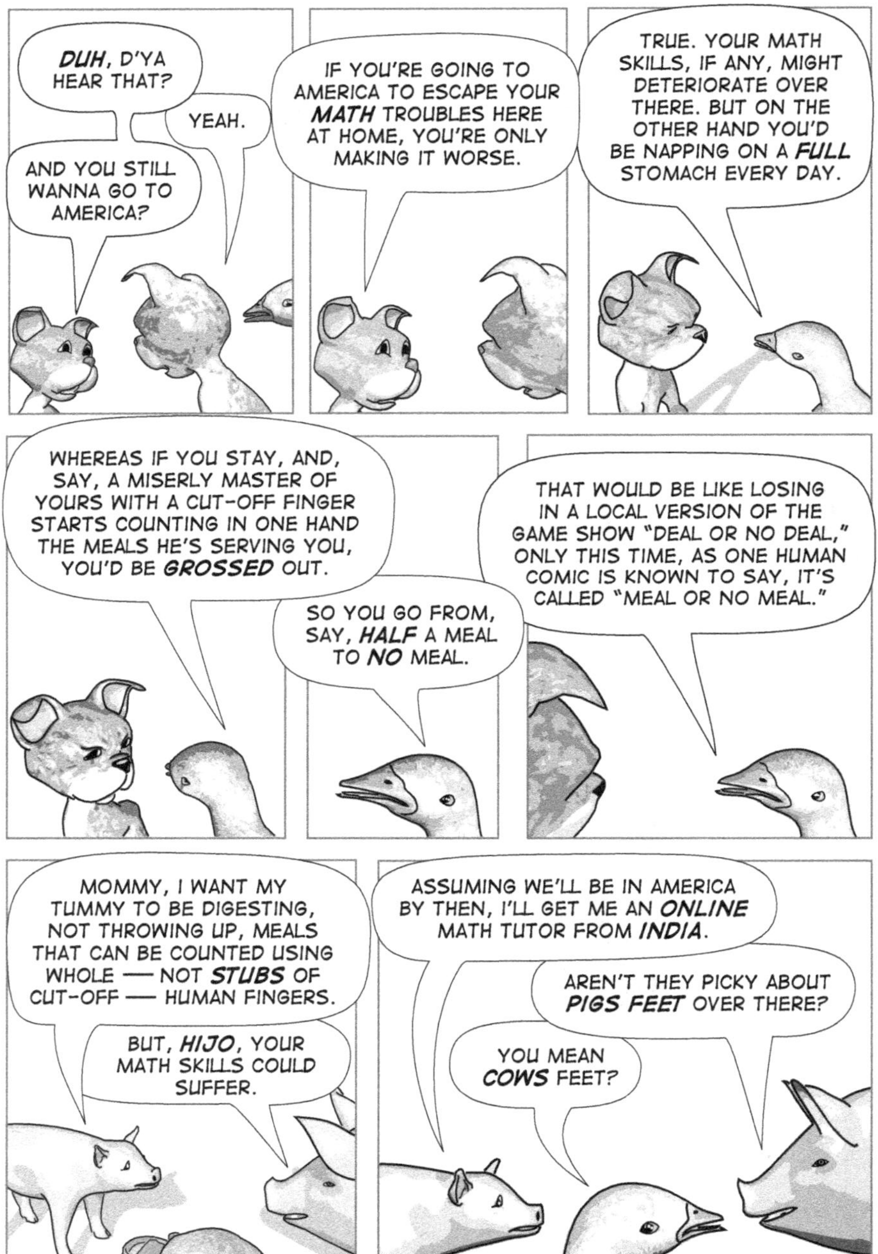
DUH, D'YA HEAR THAT?
AND YOU STILL WANNA GO TO AMERICA?
YEAH.
IF YOU'RE GOING TO AMERICA TO ESCAPE YOUR MATH TROUBLES HERE AT HOME, YOU'RE ONLY MAKING IT WORSE.
TRUE. YOUR MATH SKILLS, IF ANY, MIGHT DETERIORATE OVER THERE. BUT ON THE OTHER HAND YOU'D BE NAPPING ON A FULL STOMACH EVERY DAY.
WHEREAS IF YOU STAY, AND, SAY, A MISERLY MASTER OF YOURS WITH A CUT-OFF FINGER STARTS COUNTING IN ONE HAND THE MEALS HE'S SERVING YOU, YOU'D BE GROSSED OUT.
SO YOU GO FROM, SAY, HALF A MEAL TO NO MEAL.
THAT WOULD BE LIKE LOSING IN A LOCAL VERSION OF THE GAME SHOW "DEAL OR NO DEAL," ONLY THIS TIME, AS ONE HUMAN COMIC IS KNOWN TO SAY, IT'S CALLED "MEAL OR NO MEAL."
MOMMY, I WANT MY TUMMY TO BE DIGESTING, NOT THROWING UP, MEALS THAT CAN BE COUNTED USING WHOLE — NOT STUBS OF CUT-OFF — HUMAN FINGERS.
BUT, HIJO, YOUR MATH SKILLS COULD SUFFER.
ASSUMING WE'LL BE IN AMERICA BY THEN, I'LL GET ME AN ONLINE MATH TUTOR FROM INDIA.
AREN'T THEY PICKY ABOUT PIGS FEET OVER THERE?
YOU MEAN COWS FEET?

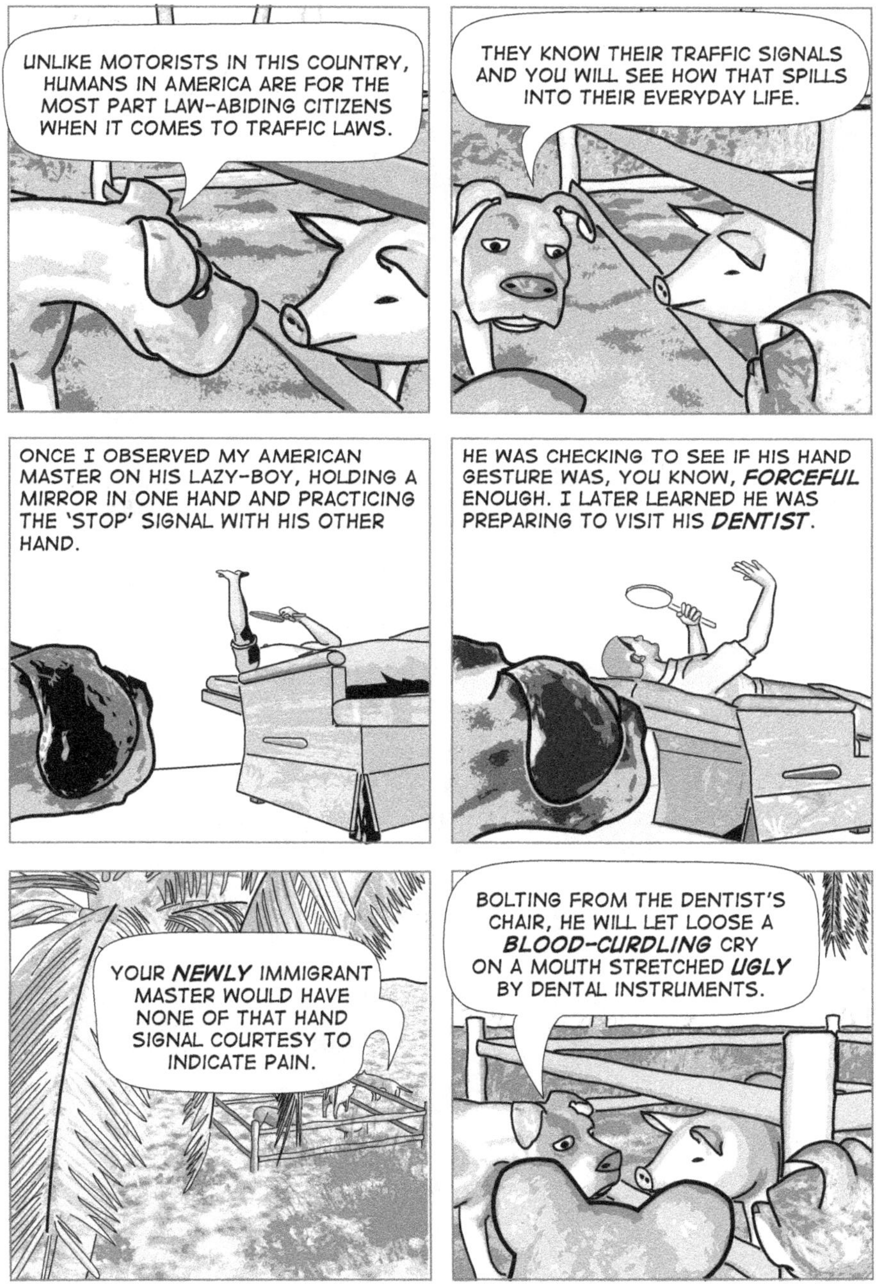
UNLIKE MOTORISTS IN THIS COUNTRY, HUMANS IN AMERICA ARE FOR THE MOST PART LAW-ABIDING CITIZENS WHEN IT COMES TO TRAFFIC LAWS.
THEY KNOW THEIR TRAFFIC SIGNALS AND YOU WILL SEE HOW THAT SPILLS INTO THEIR EVERYDAY LIFE.
ONCE I OBSERVED MY AMERICAN MASTER ON HIS LAZY-BOY, HOLDING A MIRROR IN ONE HAND AND PRACTICING THE 'STOP' SIGNAL WITH HIS OTHER HAND.
HE WAS CHECKING TO SEE IF HIS HAND GESTURE WAS, YOU KNOW, FORCEFUL ENOUGH. I LATER LEARNED HE WAS PREPARING TO VISIT HIS DENTIST.
YOUR NEWLY IMMIGRANT MASTER WOULD HAVE NONE OF THAT HAND SIGNAL COURTESY TO INDICATE PAIN.
BOLTING FROM THE DENTIST'S CHAIR, HE WILL LET LOOSE A BLOOD-CURDLING CRY ON A MOUTH STRETCHED UGLY BY DENTAL INSTRUMENTS.

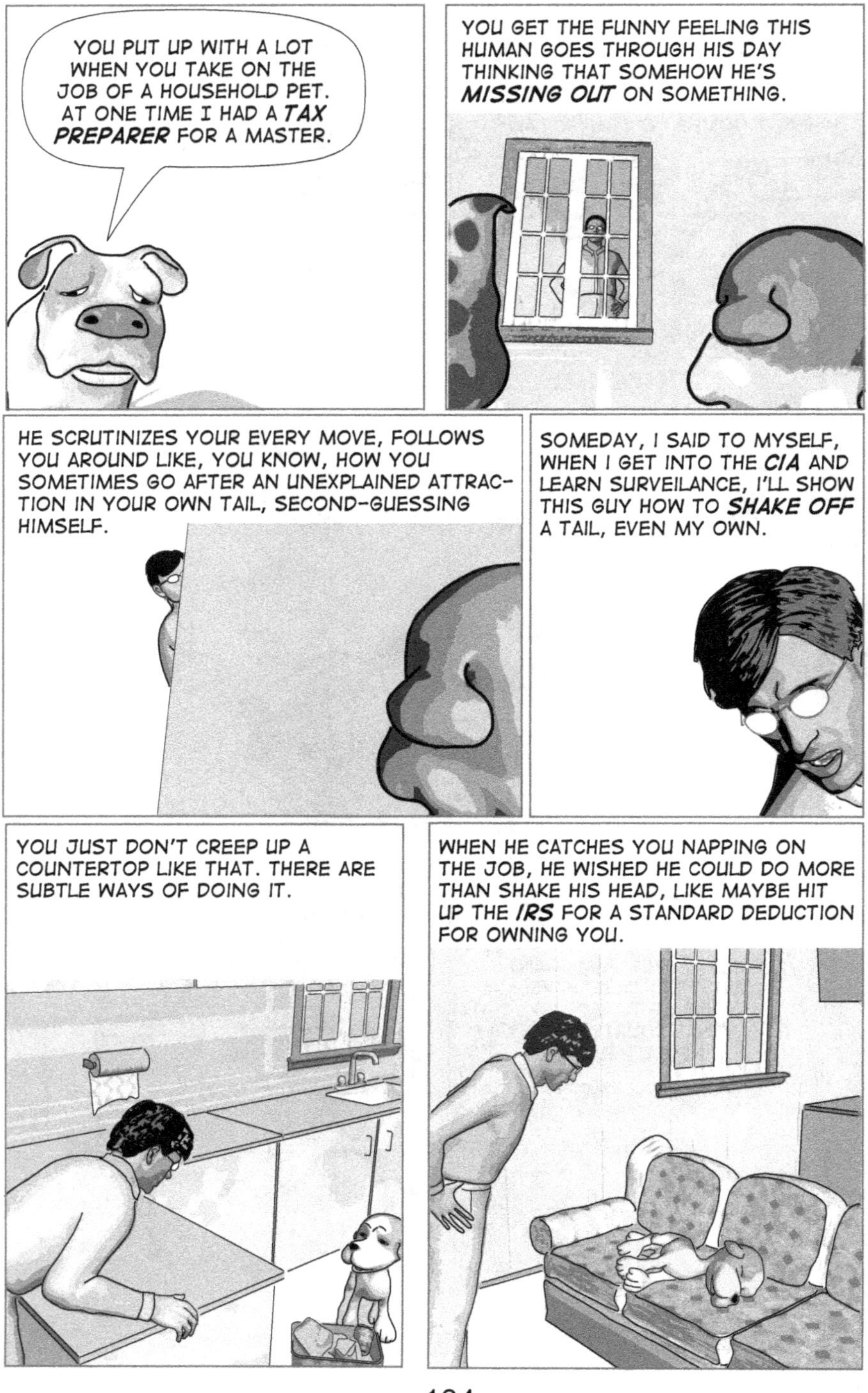
YOU PUT UP WITH A LOT WHEN YOU TAKE ON THE JOB OF A HOUSEHOLD PET. AT ONE TIME I HAD A ***TAX PREPARER*** FOR A MASTER.
YOU GET THE FUNNY FEELING THIS HUMAN GOES THROUGH HIS DAY THINKING THAT SOMEHOW HE'S ***MISSING OUT*** ON SOMETHING.
HE SCRUTINIZES YOUR EVERY MOVE, FOLLOWS YOU AROUND LIKE, YOU KNOW, HOW YOU SOMETIMES GO AFTER AN UNEXPLAINED ATTRACTION IN YOUR OWN TAIL, SECOND-GUESSING HIMSELF.
SOMEDAY, I SAID TO MYSELF, WHEN I GET INTO THE ***CIA*** AND LEARN SURVEILANCE, I'LL SHOW THIS GUY HOW TO ***SHAKE OFF*** A TAIL, EVEN MY OWN.
YOU JUST DON'T CREEP UP A COUNTERTOP LIKE THAT. THERE ARE SUBTLE WAYS OF DOING IT.
WHEN HE CATCHES YOU NAPPING ON THE JOB, HE WISHED HE COULD DO MORE THAN SHAKE HIS HEAD, LIKE MAYBE HIT UP THE ***IRS*** FOR A STANDARD DEDUCTION FOR OWNING YOU.

WITH PURSED LIPS HE CASTS A LOOK ON YOUR MEAL OF LEFTOVERS WITH AN *ITEMIZING* EYE, WONDERING IF THEY'RE *DEDUCTIBLE*.

SHOULD HE TREAT THE GARBAGE AS A GIFT TO YOU SO HE CAN CLAIM A *GIFT TAX*?

HE READS YOU LIKE HE READS A *FORENSIC* MYSTERY NOVEL, ALWAYS LOOKING FOR A *MISSING* DEDUCTION. HE NEVER BUYS DOG FOOD.

THEN WHY BOTHER WORKING FOR HIM?

THE LEFTOVERS HE SERVES ARE *FANTASTICO*. LIKE *AGING* ACCOUNTS, THEY'RE OFTEN *MORE* THAN TWO WEEKS OLD.

135

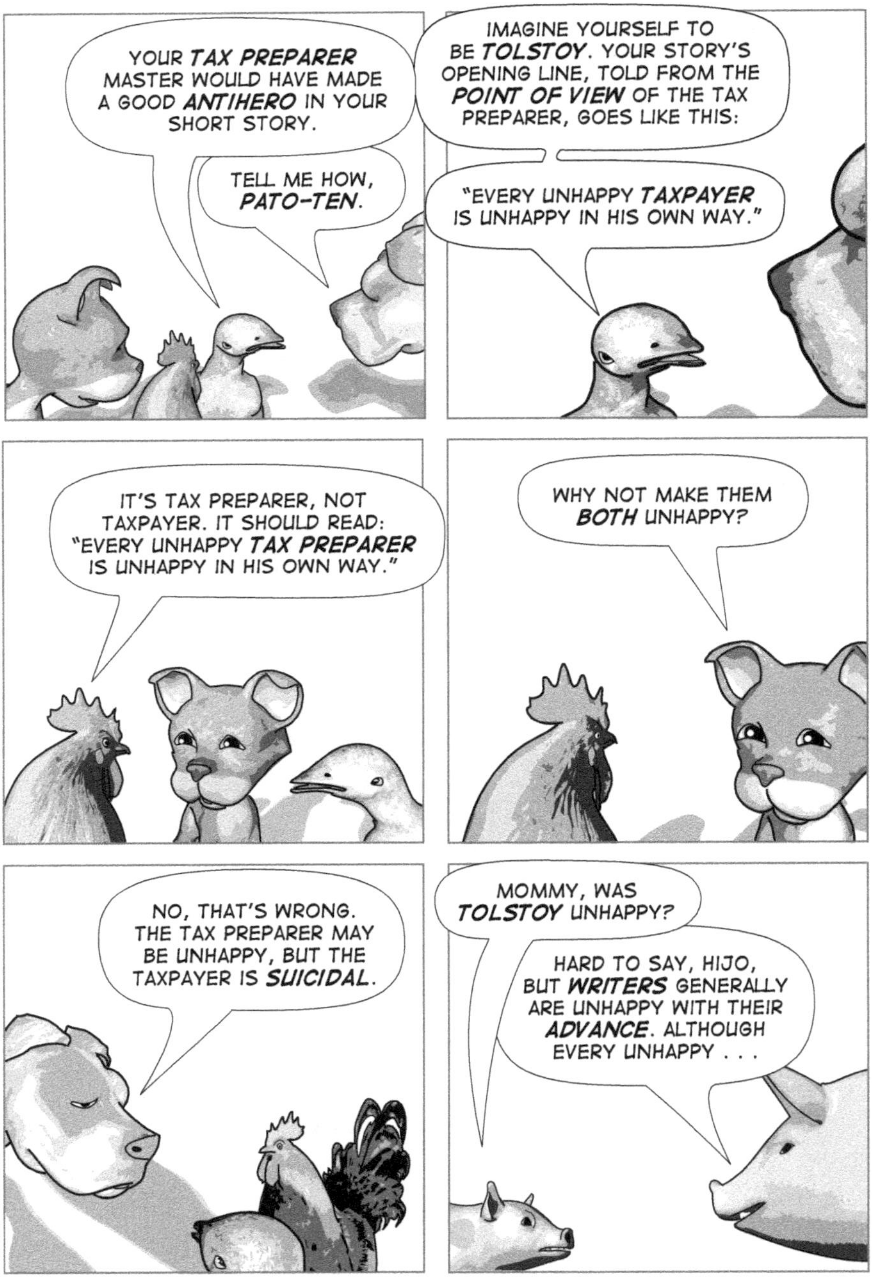
YOUR TAX PREPARER MASTER WOULD HAVE MADE A GOOD ANTIHERO IN YOUR SHORT STORY.
TELL ME HOW, PATO-TEN.
IMAGINE YOURSELF TO BE TOLSTOY. YOUR STORY'S OPENING LINE, TOLD FROM THE POINT OF VIEW OF THE TAX PREPARER, GOES LIKE THIS:
"EVERY UNHAPPY TAXPAYER IS UNHAPPY IN HIS OWN WAY."
IT'S TAX PREPARER, NOT TAXPAYER. IT SHOULD READ: "EVERY UNHAPPY TAX PREPARER IS UNHAPPY IN HIS OWN WAY."
WHY NOT MAKE THEM BOTH UNHAPPY?
NO, THAT'S WRONG. THE TAX PREPARER MAY BE UNHAPPY, BUT THE TAXPAYER IS SUICIDAL.
MOMMY, WAS TOLSTOY UNHAPPY?
HARD TO SAY, HIJO, BUT WRITERS GENERALLY ARE UNHAPPY WITH THEIR ADVANCE. ALTHOUGH EVERY UNHAPPY . . .

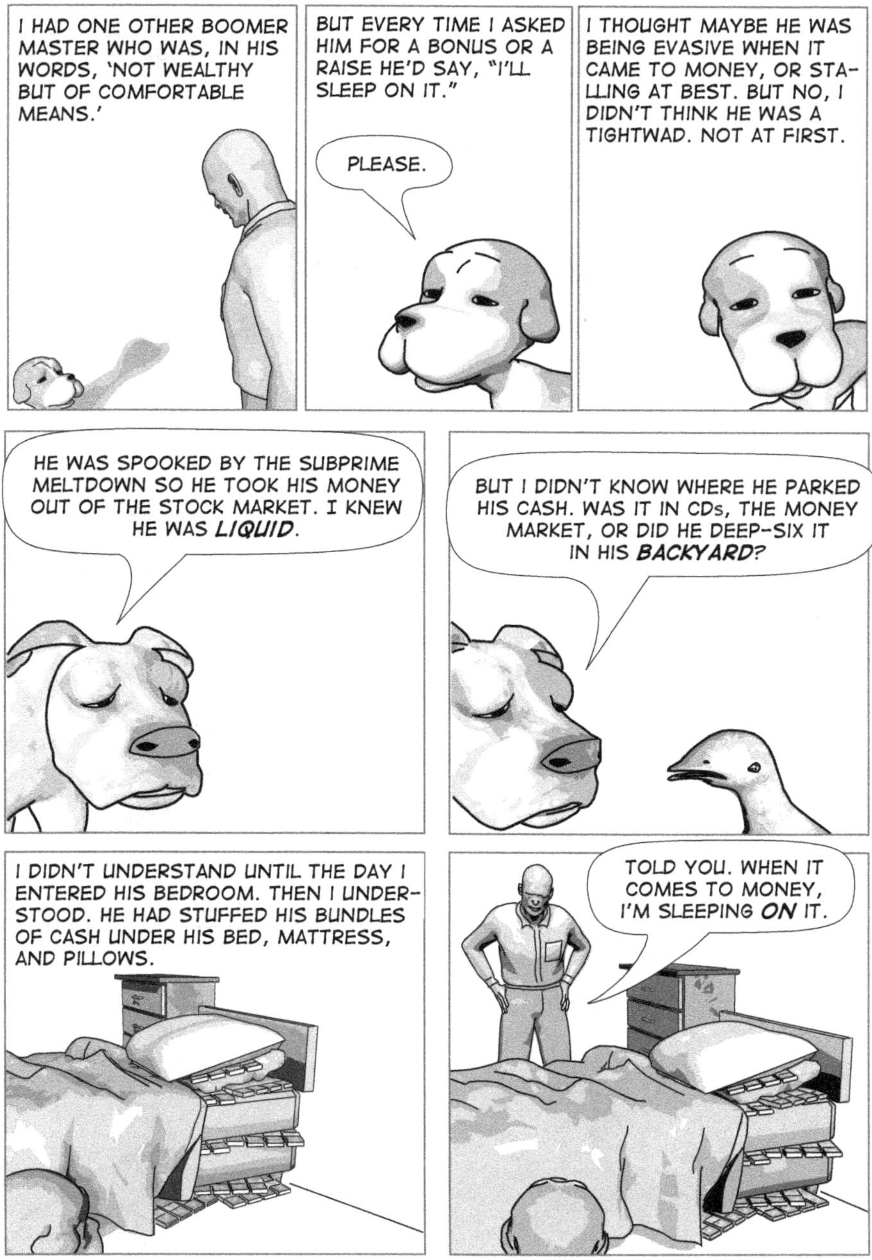
I HAD ONE OTHER BOOMER MASTER WHO WAS, IN HIS WORDS, 'NOT WEALTHY BUT OF COMFORTABLE MEANS.'
BUT EVERY TIME I ASKED HIM FOR A BONUS OR A RAISE HE'D SAY, "I'LL SLEEP ON IT."
PLEASE.
I THOUGHT MAYBE HE WAS BEING EVASIVE WHEN IT CAME TO MONEY, OR STALLING AT BEST. BUT NO, I DIDN'T THINK HE WAS A TIGHTWAD. NOT AT FIRST.
HE WAS SPOOKED BY THE SUBPRIME MELTDOWN SO HE TOOK HIS MONEY OUT OF THE STOCK MARKET. I KNEW HE WAS *LIQUID*.
BUT I DIDN'T KNOW WHERE HE PARKED HIS CASH. WAS IT IN CDs, THE MONEY MARKET, OR DID HE DEEP-SIX IT IN HIS *BACKYARD*?
I DIDN'T UNDERSTAND UNTIL THE DAY I ENTERED HIS BEDROOM. THEN I UNDERSTOOD. HE HAD STUFFED HIS BUNDLES OF CASH UNDER HIS BED, MATTRESS, AND PILLOWS.
TOLD YOU. WHEN IT COMES TO MONEY, I'M SLEEPING *ON* IT.

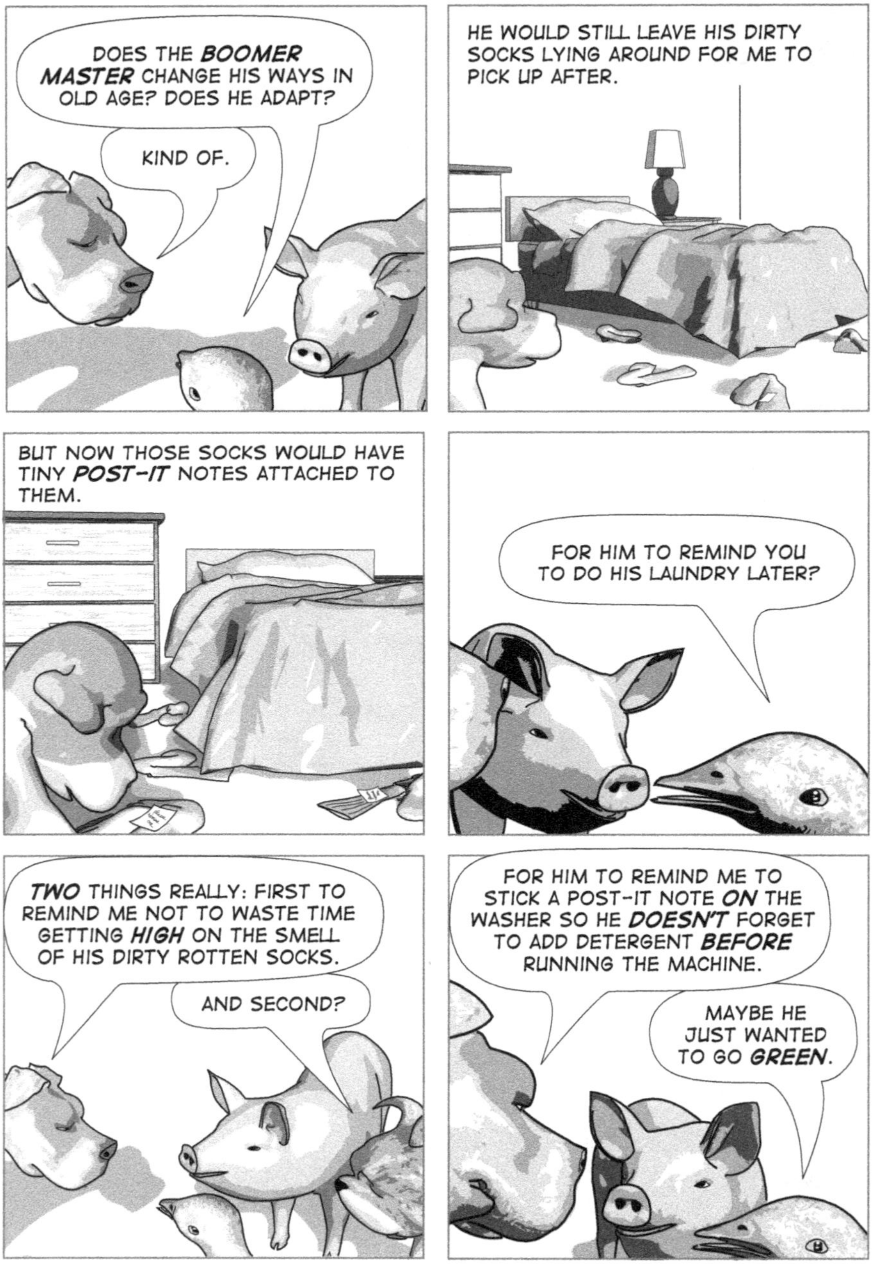
DOES THE BOOMER MASTER CHANGE HIS WAYS IN OLD AGE? DOES HE ADAPT?
KIND OF.
HE WOULD STILL LEAVE HIS DIRTY SOCKS LYING AROUND FOR ME TO PICK UP AFTER.
BUT NOW THOSE SOCKS WOULD HAVE TINY POST-IT NOTES ATTACHED TO THEM.
FOR HIM TO REMIND YOU TO DO HIS LAUNDRY LATER?
TWO THINGS REALLY: FIRST TO REMIND ME NOT TO WASTE TIME GETTING HIGH ON THE SMELL OF HIS DIRTY ROTTEN SOCKS.
AND SECOND?
FOR HIM TO REMIND ME TO STICK A POST-IT NOTE ON THE WASHER SO HE DOESN'T FORGET TO ADD DETERGENT BEFORE RUNNING THE MACHINE.
MAYBE HE JUST WANTED TO GO GREEN.

On Education

IS THERE SUCH A THING AS A MAILMAN SCHOOL IN AMERICA?
WHY DO YOU ASK?
WELL, THE WAY THE RELATIONSHIP BETWEEN A DOG AND A MAILMAN IS PORTRAYED OVER THERE, YOU WOULD THINK THERE IS SUCH A THING, JUST AS THERE IS AN OBEDIENCE SCHOOL FOR DOGS.
I'D LIKE TO THINK SO BUT I'M NOT SURE.
BUT WHAT COULD THEY POSSIBLY BE TEACHING THE LETTER CARRIERS?
PRESUMABLY, HOW TO FILE BATTERY CHARGES, ATTEND A DOG'S PAROLE HEARING, ESTIMATE THE DAMAGES FOR PAIN AND SUFFERING, . . .

DID YOU HAVE ***DISTANCE EDUCATION*** IN AMERICA?
YES, AND THAT WAS VERY POPULAR WITH MY AMERICAN DOG CLASSMATES.
25 FEET ***AWAY*** FROM THE TEACHER.
NO DOGS SAT IN THE FRONT ROWS.

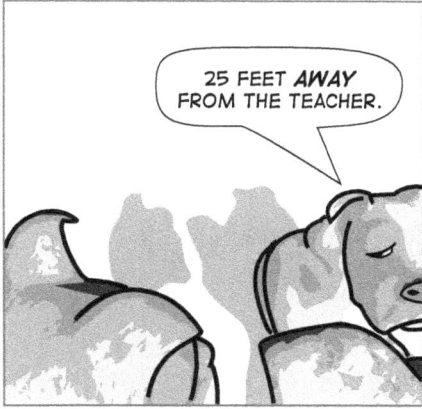

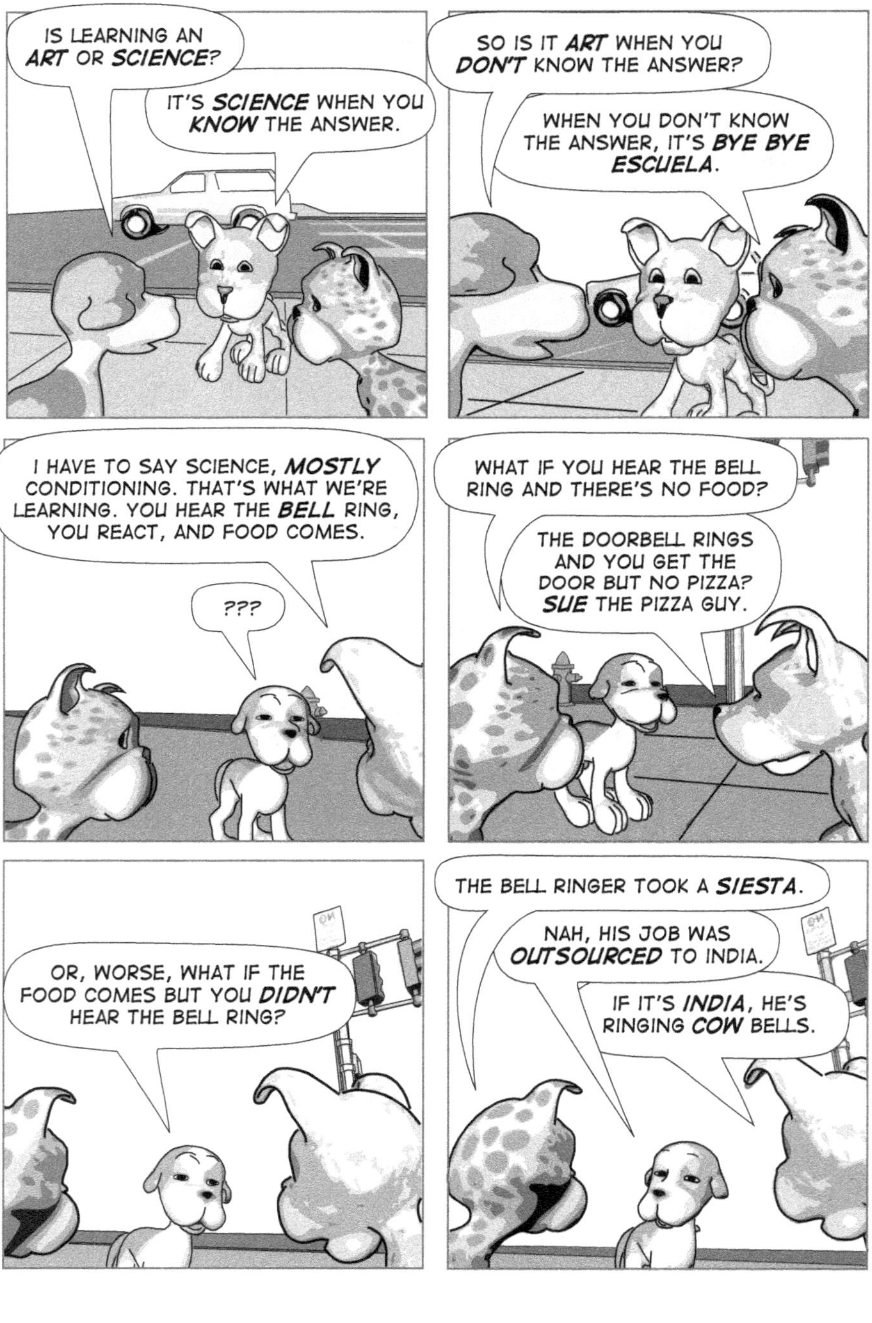
IS LEARNING AN ART OR SCIENCE?
IT'S SCIENCE WHEN YOU KNOW THE ANSWER.
SO IS IT ART WHEN YOU DON'T KNOW THE ANSWER?
WHEN YOU DON'T KNOW THE ANSWER, IT'S BYE BYE ESCUELA.
I HAVE TO SAY SCIENCE, MOSTLY CONDITIONING. THAT'S WHAT WE'RE LEARNING. YOU HEAR THE BELL RING, YOU REACT, AND FOOD COMES.
???
WHAT IF YOU HEAR THE BELL RING AND THERE'S NO FOOD?
THE DOORBELL RINGS AND YOU GET THE DOOR BUT NO PIZZA? SUE THE PIZZA GUY.
OR, WORSE, WHAT IF THE FOOD COMES BUT YOU DIDN'T HEAR THE BELL RING?
THE BELL RINGER TOOK A SIESTA.
NAH, HIS JOB WAS OUTSOURCED TO INDIA.
IF IT'S INDIA, HE'S RINGING COW BELLS.

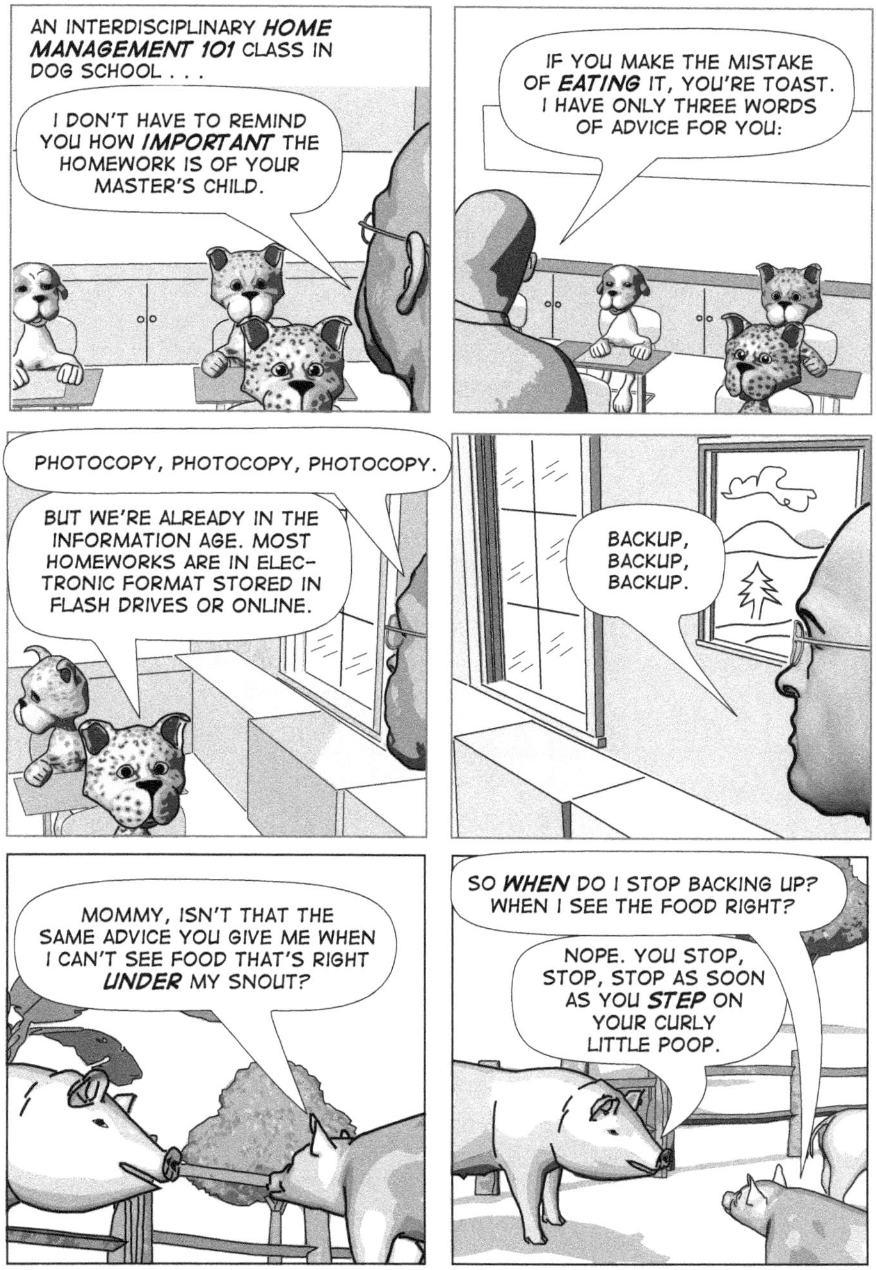
AN INTERDISCIPLINARY ***HOME MANAGEMENT 101*** CLASS IN DOG SCHOOL . . .
I DON'T HAVE TO REMIND YOU HOW ***IMPORTANT*** THE HOMEWORK IS OF YOUR MASTER'S CHILD.
IF YOU MAKE THE MISTAKE OF ***EATING*** IT, YOU'RE TOAST. I HAVE ONLY THREE WORDS OF ADVICE FOR YOU:
PHOTOCOPY, PHOTOCOPY, PHOTOCOPY.
BUT WE'RE ALREADY IN THE INFORMATION AGE. MOST HOMEWORKS ARE IN ELEC-TRONIC FORMAT STORED IN FLASH DRIVES OR ONLINE.
BACKUP, BACKUP, BACKUP.
MOMMY, ISN'T THAT THE SAME ADVICE YOU GIVE ME WHEN I CAN'T SEE FOOD THAT'S RIGHT ***UNDER*** MY SNOUT?
SO ***WHEN*** DO I STOP BACKING UP? WHEN I SEE THE FOOD RIGHT?
NOPE. YOU STOP, STOP, STOP AS SOON AS YOU ***STEP*** ON YOUR CURLY LITTLE POOP.

About the Author

   Rodolfo G Ledesma, known as "Rudy" to his friends, is an associate professor in the department of international trade at Konkuk University, Seoul, Korea, where he has taught during the past three years. In 2010 he won a Best Teacher Award from the university. A failed comedian (by his own account) before stumbling his way to Korea, Rudy has taught for a number of years at U.S. colleges and universities. Although published in scholarly journals, this is his first serious book.

www.ingramcontent.com/pod-product-compliance
Lightning Source LLC
Chambersburg PA
CBHW020501030426
42337CB00011B/185